Classics of philosophy and science
Series editor Desmond Clarke

François Poulain de la Barre

The Equality of the Sexes

Classics of philosophy and science

Series editor Desmond Clarke

G. W. Leibniz *Discourse on Metaphysics and related writings*

Edited and translated by R. Niall D. Martin and Stuart Brown

A. Arnauld *On True and False Ideas*

Translated, with an introductory essay, by Stephen Gaukroger

François Poulain de la Barre

The Equality of the Sexes

Translated with an introduction and notes by

Desmond M. Clarke

Manchester University Press

Manchester and New York

Distributed exclusively in the USA and Canada by St. Martin's Press

Published by Manchester University Press
Oxford Road, Manchester M13 9PL, UK
and Room 400, 175 Fifth Avenue,
New York, NY 10010, USA

Distributed exclusively in the USA and Canada
by St. Martin's Press, Inc.,
175 Fifth Avenue, New York, NY 10010, USA

British Library cataloguing in publication data
Poulain de la Barre, Francois
The equality of the sexes. — (Classics of philosophy and science series).
1. Sex relations
I. Title II. Series
306.7

Library of Congress cataloging in publication data applied for

ISBN 0 7190 3202 4 *hardback*

Typeset in Hong Kong
by Graphicraft Typesetters Ltd.

Printed in Great Britain
by Billing and Sons Ltd., Worcester

Contents

For Dolores

Acknowledgements

The following people have helped in various ways and made suggestions for the preparation of this translation: Jean-Pierre Cavaillé, John Cottingham, Dolores Dooley, Laurence Fontaine, Sara Matthews Grièco and Matthew MacNamara. It is a pleasure to acknowledge their contribution to the finished product.

I also wish to acknowledge the assistance of the European University Institute, Florence, which provided the context in which the translation and initial editing were completed during 1987–88.

As usual, this kind of project relied on the co-operation of various libraries and librarians in providing copies or loans of relevant material. The Bibliothèque Nationale, Paris, the British Library, and the Bibliothèque Publique et Universitaire, Geneva, provided access to original copies of Poulain's published work and other primary sources from the seventeenth century. Finally, the Arts Faculty at University College, Cork, provided financial assistance for a visit to one of these libraries and its contribution to the study is gratefully acknowledged.

Desmond M. Clarke
1 June, 1989

Note on the translation

This translation was prepared from the first edition of Poulain's text which was published in Paris in August 1673. The royal permission to publish gives the following as the full title of the book: *Discours Physique et Moral de l'Egalité des deux Sexes, où l'on voit l'Importance de se défaire des Préjugez*. The author is identified only as *Sieur P*. I have also consulted the reprinted version of the first edition which was published by Fayard (Paris, 1984), in the series: *Corpus des oeuvres de philosophie en langue française*; unfortunately this edition introduced a number of serious errors into the text which do not appear in any of the seventeenth-century editions.

In the first edition, the author provided paragraph summaries on the margin of the text; these were relegated to footnotes in subsequent editions prior to 1984. Since these short summaries do not correspond neatly to new paragraphs of the text, I have retained them in the original form as marginal headings. The division into paragraphs corresponds to the first edition.

Within sentences I have taken the liberty of changing the punctuation in a number of cases, either to restore continuity in phrases separated by a semi-colon or, more frequently, to divide a long sentence into a number of shorter ones. In attempting to be faithful to the French text and, at the same time, to provide a readable modern translation, I have translated every word in French into some English equivalent. This has some obvious disadvantages. For example, those who are familiar with the history of France under Louis XIV know that the *parlement* was not simply a court; and in using common nouns such as *honnêteté* or the corresponding adjective, *honnête*, Poulain was using words whose meaning was contested in the seventeenth century by competing theories of what constituted an *honnête* man or woman. I have not reflected the underlying complexity of these difficulties in the translation, and have opted for readability rather than scholarly diffidence. So I have not followed the maxim adopted by many translators of translating the same French term by the same word in English throughout; instead I have tried to pick the nearest word in modern English to what I think Poulain meant in different contexts. This represents a choice in favour of making Poulain's text immediately accessible to non-French readers, on the assumption that translations are usually provided for those who do not read texts in the original language.

Despite these principles of translation policy, readers may still notice mistakes or sentences which would be better rendered into English by alternative translations; if so, I would appreciate their suggestions for future correction.

Footnotes

The few notes in the original text are indicated by an asterisk and are printed as footnotes at the end of the relevant page; the translator's notes are indicated by arabic superscripts and are printed at the end of the text.

Introduction

The contribution of François Poulain de la Barre to the history of feminist thought has been eclipsed by more familiar names from the eighteenth and nineteenth centuries, such as those of William Thompson, John Stuart Mill and Mary Wollstonecraft. However there has been a resurgence of interest in Poulain in recent years, and he has eventually been recognised by many modern writers as proposing a radical egalitarian theory long before it was politically possible to implement it.[1] For this reason alone Poulain's treatise on the equality of the sexes deserves a new English translation to replace that of 1677.[2]

Poulain's contribution to the debate about the status of women is also significant for the history of philosophy, because it highlights one of the political dimensions of Cartesianism which is often neglected. The history of philosophy in seventeenth-century France and, to a great extent, in neighbouring European countries was dominated by the challenge of Descartes that philosophy and the sciences should be established on a new foundation. As long as Cartesianism is defined in terms of rather esoteric problems in metaphysics, it is difficult to appreciate the radical nature of its impact on the seventeenth century, or the intensity of the response from the established philosophy of the schools and from the defenders of religious and political orthodoxy. However, once the Cartesian method is put to work on questions which impinge on religion and politics, it is much easier to recognise its subversive influence at the time of the scientific revolution. Thus

Poulain's text deserves a wider readership as a brilliant example of how Cartesian philosophy was applied by its proponents, with a very revolutionary result, to a question which intersected with many of the religious and political controversies of the seventeenth century.

François Poulain was born in July 1647 and followed the traditional education which was prescribed for students of the priesthood.[3] He first earned a master of arts degree as a preparation for studying theology; while it is not known where he did these studies, the uniformity which was typical of seventeenth-century arts studies in France suggests that he studied a basic six-year humanities course, including Latin, and then two years of scholastic philosophy. This study was probably completed at one of the *collèges de plein exercice* in the standard course which included logic, metaphysics, physics and morals.[4] Poulain then went to study theology at the University of Paris, which would normally require a minimum of three years. His unfavourable experience of the educational system in France is reflected in his sharp criticism of the schools. Poulain's experience seems to have been typical for the time; recent historical research confirms the extent to which teaching in the colleges and the University of Paris was constrained by the categories, the method and the standard theses of the scholastic tradition. 'The professors were not only uninspired exegetes, but at the same time depressingly predictable in their conclusions. . . . Courses in the ethical and metaphysical sciences therefore filled exactly the same establishment role as a course in the humanities.' That role was one of communicating 'political and religious prejudices' to the students, and the 'brainwashing process' was most systematically applied to students of theology.[5]

It was during his theology studies that Poulain first encountered the philosophy of Descartes at one of the Cartesian study-circles at about the age of twenty, in 1667. He was converted to the merits of Descartes's approach to philosophy, just as suddenly as his more famous contemporary, Nicolas Malebranche, who was similarly won over by Cartesianism soon after his ordination to the priesthood. Poulain describes, in his *Dialogues on the Education of Women*, how he suddenly realised that everything he had studied up to that point had merely equipped him to argue in Latin in a way which no one outside the schools understood; besides, his training had prepared him for a life which no longer appealed to him.

> I realised . . . that nothing I had learned was of any use in the world except to make a living in a profession which I did not wish to follow. I saw that cultivated people could not tolerate my way of reasoning, and that I could hardly use it except in Latin, that I was completely dumbfounded if I was forced to explain myself clearly without using certain words or phrases which I imagined were sacred; . . . I could find no solution to many difficulties about things which I had previously thought were certain and very clear, . . . having studied from the age of nine to the age of twenty with a lot of dedication and success as a student, I had hardly made any more progress than if I had never begun, and I had to begin all over again . . . .[6]

It was during this period of intellectual turmoil that Poulain wrote the *The Equality of the Sexes* (1673) and, one year later, the *Dialogues on the Education of Women.*[7] Despite misgivings about his education and, it seems, about his religious faith, Poulain was ordained priest in 1680 and went to serve as a pastor in Flamangrie, in Picardie. He remained at this post for approximately eight years; then he gave up his position as *curé* and went to Paris. Poulain's departure for Paris coincided with his conversion to Calvinism. Louis XIV's France was an inhospitable place for Calvinists in the late seventeenth century; this was particularly true in the case of a Huguenot ex-priest, in the period immediately following the revocation of the Edict of Nantes in 1685. So within a few months of his arrival, Poulain left Paris again in 1688 and travelled to Geneva, where he spent the rest of his life. Poulain married in 1690 and had two children, Jeanne-Charlotte and Jean-Jacques. He survived for almost eighteen years by giving lessons in French and philosophy; he was subsequently given a teaching post at the College of Geneva and, in 1716, he was given the title of *bourgeois* by the city. He died in 1723 at the age of seventy-six.

The Equality of the Sexes was reissued in 1676, and a third edition appeared in 1679. Despite the revolutionary character of Poulain's thesis and various threats by critics to refute it, no replies to his work were published in the years immediately following 1673. So Poulain assumed the task of articulating objections to his own thesis, especially theological objections which had been almost completely ignored in his first book. These were published in 1675, *On the Superiority of Men, against the Equality of the Sexes*; although the title might suggest otherwise, this was a further defence of Poulain's original thesis about the equality of the sexes. As he explains in the Preface:

> I am surprised that after so many threats to write against the equality of the sexes, no one has done so yet, . . . That is what led me to take up my pen again to write this treatise on the superiority of men, not in order to prove that they are superior to women since I am persuaded more than ever of the opposite, but only to provide a way of comparing the two opposing views and of judging better which of them is more true.[8]

Poulain's Cartesianism and the spirit of free inquiry which it helped to cultivate affected not only his philosophical views but also his religious beliefs. His attitude to the interpretation of the Bible which is suggested by the Preface to the present book was developed in more detail in *The Protestant Doctrine of Freedom to Read Holy Scripture,* which was published in Geneva in 1720.[9] Here the author defends the right of Christians to read the Bible in the vernacular, and he argues against the Catholic doctrine of the Eucharist as a mistakenly literal reading of the words of Jesus, 'This is my Body.' Poulain's only other publication was a very small book of eighty-two pages, dedicated to one of his benefactors at Geneva, Madame Perdriau, in which he gives advice to citizens of his adopted city on the grammar and pronunciation of French.[10]

Cartesianism in Poulain de la Barre

While scholastic philosophy continued to be the dominant influence in colleges in France until the end of the seventeenth century, its intellectual hegemony was challenged by philosophical work associated with the scientific revolution. The principal exponent of the new philosophy in France was René Descartes (1596–1650). Some of Descartes's major works were published during the years when he was in exile in Holland from his native France: the *Discourse on Method and Scientific Essays* was published in 1637, the *Meditations on First Philosophy* in 1641, *The Principles of Philosophy* in 1644, and the *Passions of the Soul* in 1649. Although these works became immediately popular in the Netherlands and, to a more limited extent, in England, Descartes's philosophy had no discernible influence on the curriculum of college and university education in France during his lifetime. This situation changed significantly during the subsequent fifty-year period to the end of the century, in which the influence of Cartesianism gradually increased. Selections from Descartes's correspondence and other writings, initially edited by Claude Clerselier, were published posthumously in the years following 1657. Louis de la Forge edited Descartes's *Treatise on Man* together with his own commentary on the text in 1664, and he also published a Cartesian philosophy of mind two years later, the *Treatise on the Mind.*[11] This was followed by a series of important contributions to Cartesian philosophy which helped to popularise it in France and to accentuate the challenge to the moribund scholasticism of the schools; among those who explicitly adopted Cartesian philosophy in print were Jacques Rohault, Nicolas Malebranche, Gerauld de Cordemoy and Pierre-Sylvain Régis.[12]

To those who defended traditional scholastic philosophy, especially the Jesuits in their network of colleges throughout France, Cartesianism represented a challenge to their fundamental approach to philosophical questions. When some of Descartes's followers applied his ideas to questions about the nature of the soul or to theological doctrines about grace or the Eucharist, Cartesianism was very soon classified as heretical to the true faith. Thus some works of Descartes and Malebranche were listed in the *Index of Forbidden Books* and Catholics were forbidden to read them because they were considered dangerous to their religious faith.[13] These books were banned not only because of their actual content, but almost as much because of the association of Cartesianism with Jansenism in France and, on the other hand, its spirit of free enquiry which aligned it too closely with Calvinism. From the point of view of Rome — a perspective shared for partly political reasons by Louis XIV — Cartesianism smacked of the Protestant reformation and of Catholic fundamentalism!

This raises a question about the spirit of Cartesian philosophy which apparently earned it so many opponents almost as soon as it began to be publicised in France. Rather than attempt to summarise Cartesian philosophy, it may help to list a few of the Cartesian themes which were adapted by Poulain and which were exploited with telling effect in *The Equality of the Sexes*.

(a) *Authority and reason*: One of the most fundamental ideas in Cartesian philosophy is that the authority of those who teach is irrelevant in comparison with the reasons they might offer in support of their philosophical or scientific theories. This is a theme which runs right through Cartesianism, especially when confronting the authoritarian philosophy of the schools. Of course it was not a feature of Aristotle's or Plato's philosophy that something was true because some famous person said so, and it would not have been asserted in this blunt form even by scholastic philosophers in the seventeenth century. However, the authority attributed to the ancients or to scholastic interpretations of Greek and medieval philosophy was so great that theories which differed from them or challenged them were almost automatically considered to be false. In this sense, scholastic philosophers attributed a degree of authority to their understanding of ancient authors which made it close to impossible to challenge their views on a whole range of questions from astronomy, medicine and biology to the nature of the mind or the relation between religious faith and reason.

Cartesians proposed substituting reason or, in slightly different terms, common sense or sound judgement for the authority of the ancients and denying any weight to arguments which depended on the identity of their proponents or the length of time during which such arguments had been accepted. Ultimately, each individual must rely on his or her own judgement and make up their mind on the major issues which were disputed by theologians or philosophers.

(b) *Sense knowledge and prejudice*: It was a standard thesis of the scientific revolution in the seventeenth century — which was expounded by Descartes among others — that we cannot trust our sensations as reliable guides to the truth about objective reality. We are not justified in projecting our perceptions on to reality, on the assumption that there is always something in reality which corresponds to the way in which we perceive things. This was the famous distinction between so-called primary and secondary qualities; in the example used both by Galileo and Descartes, there is nothing in a feather — for example, something like an objective tickle — which corresponds to our sensation of tickling. The sensation of tickling which we experience when stroked by a feather is a perception of a secondary quality; however, there is nothing outside our minds which could be described properly as a tickle. The only primary or objective qualities involved in causing a tickling sensation are the motion of the feather in contact with our skin, its shape, softness, etc. In contrast, the qualitative features of the perception of tickling result from human consciousness.

One of the ways in which Cartesians constantly reminded their readers of this thesis was by reference to the spontaneous mistaken beliefs of children. Children are not sophisticated enough to realise that reality may not correspond to their perceptions; and scholastic philosophers were described as falling into the same mistake as children whenever they trust their sensations as guides to the truth.

It is in this sense that Descartes argued, in a famous section of the *Meditations*, that our senses deceive us; we cannot assume that objective reality corresponds exactly to the way in which we perceive it. Another way of expressing the same insight was to describe as prejudices or pre-judgements our spontaneous, unreflective judgements based on perceptions of the way in which reality appears to us. In Poulain's definition, prejudices are 'judgements which are made without due caution and without examining (what is at issue), or those beliefs, opinions or maxims which are adopted without discernment'.[14]

By generalising the theory of primary and secondary qualities to all instances of uncritical perception Poulain was able to argue that, in considering the question of the equality of the sexes, we are deceived if we unreflectively accept our perception of women's current condition as a basis for judging their innate capacities.

(c) *Clear and distinct ideas*: If we reject the authority of the ancients and if we are appropriately sceptical of how things seem to our uncritical perceptions, what can we turn to in order to make up our minds about disputed issues? The slogan invented by Descartes to describe his method for discovering the truth was 'clear and distinct ideas', and this is adopted by Poulain at the very beginning of his work. What are clear and distinct ideas?

Descartes's explicit comments on his formula are not very helpful. Basically it referred to the method which was expounded in his *Discourse on Method* and which was implemented in various forms to resolve problems ranging from astronomy and geometry to metaphysics and music. Adopting the traditional distinction between analysis and synthesis, Descartes proposed that we should analyse complex problems into simple, manageable sub-problems; that we should analyse concepts almost in the way in which twentieth-century analytic philosophy became devoted to conceptual analysis; that we should establish basic metaphysical categories which would underpin our whole cognitive enterprise (see (d) below); and when trying to resolve empirical or scientific questions, we should be guided by careful observations and experiments. In simple terms, this was a method for sifting through the evidence which allegedly supports any position or theory, and then trying to gauge the extent to which it is credible on the basis of our examination of the evidence rather than on what some teaching authority, lay or clerical, may have said about it.

(d) *Matter and mind*: One of the first fruits of Descartes's analysis of concepts was a complete separation of the concepts of matter and spirit (or mind). In Descartes's metaphysics, matter was defined in such a way that it had nothing in common with mind, and vice versa. The sharp distinction between mind and matter implied that we should avoid ambiguity in classifying things as spiritual or material; everything has to be either one or the other, and there is nothing in between. If something is spiritual, then by definition it is a thinking substance or it belongs to a thinking substance as one of its modes; if it is a material thing, then it cannot think and all its properties must be explained mechanically. This uncompromising attitude gave rise to the famous Cartesian theory of animal machines, to which Poulain refers in Part I, according to which non-human animals have no spiritual or mental dimension; all their perceptions, behaviour, etc., can be explained by analogy with clocks or similar complex machines.

Another implication which is more central to Poulain's project is that our minds are spiritual substances which are not in any way to be confused with or identified with our bodies. Thus our minds obviously have no sexual characteristics, and one mind (whether of a man or woman) is just as competent as any other mind to discover the truth. If there are differences between individuals, or even between the sexes, in their native ability to discover the truth then those differences must be explained by some other factors apart from the innate capacities of the human mind.

(e) *Experimental science*: The conceptual distinction between matter and mind coincided with a disciplinary distinction between physical sciences (such as optics or medicine) and metaphysics. Here again Cartesianism provided support for Poulain's thesis. Since the souls or minds of men and women are identical, the only possible basis for claims about their inequality would be physical differences in their bodies. Cartesians argued that we cannot understand the human body without studying anatomy and physiology, and that these are necessarily experimental disciplines. So in contrast to the practice of medical studies in Poulain's time, in which students studied the reported views of Galen or Aristotle, Descartes argued that we can understand how the body functions only by detailed observations of its functioning. Hence the relevance of Descartes's physiological works, some of which were edited by the Saumur physician, Louis de la Forge, and published in 1664. This empirical attitude left Cartesians with only one option with respect to the equality of the sexes. They could claim that women were superior or inferior to men only if their bodies could be shown to be superior or inferior to those of men in some specified respect. Thus someone could claim that women were less suitable for scientific work because their brains were inferior to those of men, as Malebranche suggested without any supporting evidence;[15] alternatively, one could claim like Poulain that physiologists had found no significant difference between the brains of men and women and therefore women must have the same intellectual capacities as men.

(f) *Hypotheses*: Cartesianism was the primary supporter in France of a hypothetical approach to explaining natural phenomena. Since natural phenomena are explicable, according to Descartes, only by reference to the imperceptible particles which combine to form any physical body, we can do no better than imagine some combination of these particles which would give rise to whatever observable effects we hope to explain. In other words, scientific explanations are always hypothetical. The logic of hypothetical explanations was adapted from problems in physics to other disciplines, including history. Thus if a

Cartesian wished to explain the present inferior condition of women in society, it is perfectly in keeping with Cartesian method to formulate an historical hypothesis, an invented reconstruction of past events, which might causally result in current historical realities. Poulain does this explicitly in constructing his historical hypothesis; he does so less explicitly in attempting to identify the reasons why women continued to be denied equality in seventeenth-century France despite the fact that, both from the point of view of their bodies and their minds, they are at least equal to men in the relevant capacities for most professions or civil offices. Poulain's explanation of the inferior status of women should be read as a typical Cartesian hypothesis designed to explain rationally an observed social phenomenon.

These themes were exploited by all those who adopted Descartes's philosophy in the seventeenth century, even if they applied them to different problems or if they used them to argue for different results. Poulain had read not only Descartes but other French Cartesians such as La Forge and Cordemoy; he was ideally placed, therefore, to apply Cartesianism to the question of the equality or otherwise of men and women and to make a novel contribution to a debate which had already been initiated in France by less philosophically gifted predecessors.

Feminism in seventeenth-century France

Poulain's work should be read in the context of an ongoing debate, both in France and more generally in Europe in the sixteenth and seventeenth centuries, concerning the role of women in society and their equality or otherwise with men. In the hundred-year period immediately prior to Poulain's publication, controversy about women — the so-called *querelle des femmes* — included a number of overlapping themes: the value of marriage compared with celibacy, courtly love compared with other kinds of love between the sexes, the virtues and social graces of a lady (a *femme honnête*), and the education of women for the limited roles which were envisaged for them. These themes were expressed in distinctive literary genres which extolled the superiority of women or depicted images of heroic women, and in moralistic tracts on marriage and women's place in society; in some cases writers expressed their views on women's issues more for the entertainment of their readers than for any more serious purpose.[16]

The mutual reinforcing of theological, philosophical and medical theories about women which emerged in this debate appears, in retrospect, to be nothing more than a widespread rationalisation on the part of men for keeping women in the inferior position to which they had been subjected. There is a typical expression of how, for example, women's intelligence was regarded as innately inferior to that of men, in *The Praise of Folly* by Erasmus:

> For where Plato is uncertain whether to place women among rational or irrational creatures, he intended no more than to point out the extraordinary folly of that sex. And if by chance a woman should wish to be considered wise, she simply shows that she is twice foolish, since she is attempting something 'completely against the grain', as they say, like someone bringing 'a bull to a chinashop'. For a fault is redoubled if someone tries to gloss it over with unnatural disguises and to work against the inborn bias of the mind. The Greek proverb says 'An ape is still an ape, even if it is dressed up in royal purple'; just so, a woman is still a woman — that is, a fool — no matter what role she may try to play.[17]

When one considers the extent to which naked misogyny was institutionalised in witch-trials and the frequency with which women were tortured and publicly burned as witches, especially during the early part of the seventeenth century, it is difficult to see how people could have been persuaded even to consider changing their views about a situation which allegedly resulted from God's creation (nature) and was compounded by Original Sin.[18] Yet this is exactly what happened in the course of the debate, in which contributors defended the superiority of women, the equality of women and, more generally, the inferiority of women to men.

One can get a good idea of the style of the debate and of the merits of contrasting positions from a tract written by Jacques Olivier in 1617, *An Alphabet of the Imperfection and Malice of Women.*

> Woman! If your arrogant and fickle mind could understand the fate of your misery and the vanity of your condition, you would flee from the light of day and seek out the shadows, you would hide in caverns and caves, you would curse your misfortune, regret your birth and hate yourself. However the extreme blindness which has taken away this knowledge makes you live in society as the most imperfect creature of the universe, the scum of nature, the breeding ground of misfortune, the source of controversy, the laughing stock of the insane, the scourge of wisdom, the firebrand of Hell, the instigator of vice, the cesspool of filth, a monster in nature, a necessary evil, a multiform chimera, a harmful pleasure, the bait of the Devil, the enemy of the Angels, the mask of God, deforming and undermining the wisdom of the very God who created you.[19]

Beginning with his dedication to the 'worst creature in the world', Olivier writes a lengthy book which is arranged alphabetically in sections (starting with 'A', for 'a very avaricious animal'), and which is designed to list all the vices which are characteristic of women. When a certain Mr Vigoureux was bold enough to defend women against Olivier's charges[20] — claiming that all the faults attributed to women are more evident in men and and that women's faults all derive from men in the first place — Olivier replied in the same year:

> It is said, and it is true, that it is not the business of a blind man to judge colours; I say that it is not the business of an ignorant soldier like you to criticize and reproach those who prove their claims with good arguments and by reference to authorities drawn from Holy Scripture and reliable authors, both philosophers and theologians.[21]

Olivier completely dismisses the attempted reply of someone whom he calls a 'poor idiot' and 'an effeminate captain'.[22]

The polarised positions adopted by these two authors were typical of a very wide literature on the status of women. It included, on the one hand, those who argued that women were the source of all manner of evil and were created 'inferior to man, whom God has given them as their head, their prince and their lord, as the Apostle says: *man is the head of woman*';[23] it also included, at the opposite extreme, those who argued for the superiority of women and exaggerated their virtues. There is a typical example of the first position in Rolet, *Historical Table of the Wiles and Craftiness of Women* (1623), which claims that 'the fickleness of women and the variations in their moods is the exclusive source of evils which occur in this world'.[24] And, defending the opposite position, one finds François Du Soucy, *The Triumph of Women* (1646) and Jacquette Guillaume, *Illustrious Women: or it is proved by sound and convincing reasons that the female sex surpasses the male sex in all kinds of things* (1665).[25] The style of those supporting women seems, in retrospect, to have been as excessive as the contemptuous presentation of those who adopted Olivier's attitude. For example, Gabriel Gilbert wrote as follows, in his *Panegyric to Women* (1650):

> I planned to show that women are more perfect than men, ... It is not a question here of one person, or one town, or of just one kingdom, but of half the human race which rivals the other half for superiority. ... When I look back in my memory on all the centuries, on all the illustrious women there have been and all the memorable things they have done, it is easy for me to find arguments and evidence in their favour. The only thing which causes problems is making a choice; it is the abundance of evidence rather than its meagreness which stops me. Beauty, grace, knowledge and the virtues come forward in a flood; they come to inspire me with what I should say in praise of ladies, and to spread out at the feet of your Royal Majesty [i.e. the regent, Anne of Austria] the flowers from which I should make their crowns. In order to give them all the praise which they deserve, I will show that they not only surpass men in the perfection of their bodies, but

> that they are also superior in intellectual gifts. Nature, in forming such a perfect sex, chose what was most pure and exquisite from the elements and mixed their rare qualities with the most sweet powers of the heavens; it is from this noble composition and the perfect blending of these things that there results the beauty of women, the bright colours of their complexion, the red of their lips, and the light of their eyes. They also have majesty in their bearing, grace in action, and sweetness in their voice; and all their perfections are gifts which are peculiar to them, and ones in which our sex has hardly any share at all. . . . Despite this, there are some men who have the audacity to claim that women are inferior to them in many things, and especially in the sciences. But despite what they say, women have more ability in the sciences than men, and their discourse would reveal the quality of their minds if they did not try to hide their knowledge as much as we try to show off ours.[26]

The same style of flowery exaggeration is apparent in the more well-known book by François Du Soucy, *The Triumph of Women* (1646):

> I claim with a lot of justification that, if men are convinced that they have some advantage over women, that is nevertheless without foundation, for nature has denied men a thousand excellent qualities with which it has adorned women in order to make them the most perfect creatures in the world. One would have to be blind and lacking in judgment not to value their beauty, their grace and their attractions. It would be barbaric to deny them so many marvellous qualities which they have. . . . And I think that no one can deny that God has created them so perfectly as the masterpiece of nature. . . . Since God planned from eternity to create the world by a very admirable order of his providence, he decided that some creatures should depend on certain others, that the inferior ones would be subject to the superior; and having made them all for man's sake, he subsequently created man and gave him complete power over them all. However having created man, he wished to give him a companion, which he made not

> just equal to him, but he wished that she would surpass him in the beauty of her body and her mind.
>
> Women: This treatise was written to prove that your gifts are superior to those of men; and to show that even the most learned are not as enlightened as you are; I should not be ashamed to claim (as I do) that what you deserve is way above the limits of my eloquence, and that I found much greater difficulty in describing your eminent virtues than you have in practising them.[27]

Apart from the competing claims about women's alleged superiority or inferiority to men, there were numerous contributors to the discussion of the virtues proper to women and, more generally, of the ideal of propriety summarised in the term '*honnête*'. P. Du Bosc was typical of this genre, in writing *L'Honneste Femme* (1632), as was François de Grenaille's *L'Honneste Fille* (1640).[28] One should include in the same category those who wrote about the moral law on marriage, such as Moise Amiraut, *Considerations on the laws by which nature has regulated marriage* (1648).[29]

There was a variant of this genre in books which gave accounts of the exploits of famous women and of the virtues they displayed in their heroic deeds. For example, Pierre le Moyne published *The Gallery of Great Women* (1647) which comprised a series of drawings of famous women, many from the Old Testament and, associated with each one in turn, a discussion of the extent to which women may acquire virtues such as bravery, constancy, wisdom, etc. In general, Le Moyne opts for a compromise on most issues, arguing that women are not incapable of governing or of studying, but that custom dictates the role which society has devised for women and that they can exercise heroic virtue within the confines of their traditional roles.

> One cannot say that women are absolutely incapable of governing; . . . states are not governed with a beard, nor by the austerity of one's face; they are governed by the strength of mind and the power and skill of reason.

> The mind can be as strong and reason as powerful and skilful in the head of a woman as in that of a man ... apart from superficial differences which do not affect the soul, nor cause an inequality among minds. ... Women should hold to the distribution of roles which nature and law has made and which custom has inherited; and they should be satisfied with the role which was assigned to them in the economy and the home.[30]

This genre of writing in praise of heroic women and their virtues is also exemplified in books such as Louis Machon's *A Discourse or Apologetic Lecture in Support of Women* (1641), or Madeleine de Scudery's *Illustrious Women* (1642).[31]

Finally, among all the controversy about the role of women in society and their natural inferiority or superiority, there emerged a new line of argument in the claim that men and women were equal. This was the thesis of Marie de Jars de Gournay (1565–1654). She was born in Picardie and read Montaigne's *Essays* at the age of eighteen. She subsequently went to Paris, where she met Montaigne in 1588 and later collaborated with him in preparing a second edition of the *Essays*. Marie de Gournay had two short tracts published in the early seventeenth century: her *Equality of Men and Women* was published in 1622, and four years later *Women's Grievance* appeared.[32] She argued that women were equal to men: 'The human being is neither man nor woman when understood properly, since the sexes are not created as such but, as the schools express it, *secundum quid* [from a certain point of view], that is to say, only for propagation. The unique form and specific difference of this animal is found only in the human soul.'[33] In other words, sexual characteristics are merely accidental features or qualities which do not affect the common nature which is identical in men and women. As in the case of the slightly later Dutch feminist, Anne-Marie Schurman, Marie de Gournay relied on Aristotelian categories and traditional arguments to defend her thesis on the equality of the sexes. She also argued that since women's nature was equal to that of men, at least in respect of intellectual abilities, the unequal status of women must be explained in terms of their unequal education.

Whether or not women could be educated in the same way as men, and whether they should be educated in this way, was a central theme of the seventeenth-century debate about women; the various views held on this question reflected their authors' views on the more substantive question of equality. Those who argued for the superiority of women also claimed, like Du Soucy, that:

> they have a natural liveliness which makes them understand easily whatever natural objects they encounter. They have an excellent memory, and they reason with so much care that their judgements, on many issues, are often taken as laws of the mind by those who are most learned. And one must surely agree that the mind of women is incomparably more pleasant than that of men, and the sweetness of their conversation is always the best school for the most polite people.[34]

Thus women's minds were regarded as superior to those of men or, for defenders of the opposite position, they were naturally inferior and there was no point in educating women at all.

The compromise position on women's education, corresponding to the revised ideal of an '*honnête femme*', was expressed by a number of authors who argued that women should get some education to prepare them for their evolving role in society, but that it should be devoted primarily to cultivating the virtues which were proper to a woman. For example Du Bosc agreed that, on condition that they avoid excessive study, ladies who have some knowledge or have done some reading improve the quality of their conversation;[35] and Louis de Lesclache, in *The Benefits which Women can Gain from Philosophy and especially from Ethics* (1667), advised that women should not study school philosophy, nor should they attempt to study the new natural philosophy made popular by the Cartesians, because both would distract them from their role in society, would lead to vanity and eventually imperil their eternal salvation.

> Women should not apply themselves to studying physics, looking for a new world on the moon, . . . or doing many experiments to weigh air, or to defend or oppose a vacuum, because these researches and many others of the same type are unworthy of the pursuit of a genuine philosopher; but they should draw from physics a knowledge of their soul, in order to raise themselves to a knowledge of God. . . . Women who would like to apply themselves to studying physics should know that whoever seeks knowledge of all natural things is in danger of working in vain, of falling into many errors, and of raising himself against God by his vanity.[36]

The claim to equality of opportunity in education was forcefully presented by Anne Marie Schurman in *A Famous Question: Whether it is Necessary or not for Girls to be Learned* (1646).[37] Despite her contribution in arguing that women have as much need of learning as men and in demonstrating by her renowned learning that it was possible for women to do as she recommended, her work fell on deaf ears and was generally ignored. This can be seen in an apparently sympathetic work written towards the end of the century, Fénelon's *Treatise on the Education of Girls* (1687); on first reading this might seem to be a vindication of the right of women to access to education on an equal footing with men.[38] However a closer reading of the text shows that it was nothing of the sort; Fénelon's pedagogical proposals for women were inspired by a twofold conservative reaction to what he saw or feared might develop in the France of Louis XIV. He opposed the introduction of women into polite society and, in general, their exposure to all the excesses which were associated with the royal court. For this reason he advocated that women should avoid luxury, vanity, and the life of the salons. Secondly, he opposed the more radical thesis which had been proposed by Poulain, that women should have access on a par with men to all offices or professions in society; for Fénelon, 'A woman's intellect is normally more feeble and her curiosity greater than those of a man; also it is undesirable to set her to studies which may turn her head. Women should not govern the state or make war or enter the sacred ministry.'[39] What was left for women was an improved version of the inferior, domestic role which had been traditionally available to them; given the complexity of even that role in late seventeenth-century France, women's studies were designed by Fénelon to equip them to fulfil this traditional role by teaching them how to manage their households, to supervise servants, to buy and sell, to keep accounts, etc.

> We come now to the details of those matters in which a woman should be instructed. What are her occupations? She has the duty of educating her children — the boys up to a certain age and girls until they get married or take the veil. She has the supervision of the servants, with their manners and duties. She must see to the details of household expenditure and to the means of doing everything economically and honourably; and usually she must also look after leases and the receiving of rents. The limits of a woman's learning — like those of a man — should be determined by her duties. The difference in their studies should be conditioned by the difference in their occupations. A woman's instruction therefore should be restricted to the matters which we have mentioned.[40]

In a word, it was an early version of domestic science; and while women were being thus trained for higher productivity in the home, they were also trained to overcome all the stereotyped vices which Fénelon recognised in them, such as jealousy, vanity, cunning, idleness, etc.![41] There was no suggestion that educational reform might be used to change women's place in society; rather the status quo was to determine the kind of education which women should get.

This programme of educating girls was implemented by Madame de Maintenon when the *Maison royale de Saint Louis* at Saint-Cyr was founded in 1686. This school was designed to wean girls away from the attractions of polite society and to train them to be good, obedient wives of the nobility. Hence girls were not encouraged to read too much because it would make them insubordinate; nor did they need to write, or study languages. Above all they needed to learn the role of a faithful, obedient, virtuous wife and to play the role which had been assigned to each woman by nature and by her social status.

The paternalistic conservatism of Saint-Cyr was the very antithesis of equality for women in education; it had little in common with Poulain's theory that women should be integrated as equal partners with men in all the professions and, as a prerequisite, that they should have access to the same educational facilities as men.

Poulain's feminism

Poulain's feminism is elegant in its simplicity and radical in its conclusions. He directly confronts the question: whether the unequal status of women results from their nature or from human institutions and custom.

The allegedly *natural* basis of women's inequality was cited by a wide variety of writers who reflected the opinions of their own time. For example, Erasmus wrote in *On the Education of Children* that 'it is contrary to nature that a woman should rule over men. Nothing is more cruel than the opposite sex once its anger has been aroused; its passions are easily kindled and are quietened only when the lust for revenge has been satisfied.'[42] This comment appears in a context in which Erasmus advises fathers not to send their sons to be taught by a drunkard of a man; *a fortiori*, it is even worse to send a boy for tuition to 'an incompetent, drunken female, for this is against nature'. In a similarly dogmatic style Jean Bodin claimed, in his *Six Books of the Commonwealth* (1576), that is is against the law of nature that women should rule; besides, the law of God also ordains that women should be subject to men.

> I have said that the crown ought to descend in the male line, seeing that gynecocracy is directly contrary to the laws of nature. Nature has endowed men with strength, foresight, pugnacity, authority, and has deprived women of these qualities. Moreover the law of God implicitly enjoins that the woman should be sub-

> ject, not only in matters concerning law and government, but within each particular family.[43]

Erasmus or Bodin were unexceptional in their appeal to the law of nature; it was commonly taught by the learned and generally believed by the educated and uneducated alike that women's inferior status resulted from God's plan as expressed in nature, the work of his creation.

Poulain rejects the argument from nature and suggests instead that people have confused nature and custom. Thus lawyers use the law to subject women to men, and 'then say that it is nature which assigned the lowest functions in society to women' (p. 82); they attribute 'to nature a distinction which derives only from custom' (p. 82), although it is clear that lawyers would be hard pressed even to explain what they mean by the term 'nature' in this context. Ordinary people make the same mistake and 'confuse nature and custom' when they spontaneously assume that people's varying aptitudes must derive from their nature. Medical doctors are confused when they fail to differentiate 'what derives from custom and education from what is due to nature' (p. 116). In general, from the mere fact that women do not exercise most of the important functions or offices in civil society or in the churches, we cannot draw the conclusion that they must be inferior to men in some natural respect. How should we analyse the current situation, then, and what conclusions are we justified in drawing?

Here Poulain's radical Cartesianism comes into play. What he considers a misinterpretation of observable data derives from two sources: the authority of famous men, and the Scriptures. 'As regards the first of these, I think that I can answer them satisfactorily by saying that I recognise no authority apart from the authority of reason and of sound judgement' (p. 44). So in place of the deferential quoting of ancient authorities, Poulain challenges readers to examine the evidence themselves, to apply Cartesian method to the question at issue, and then make up their minds on the basis of the evidence. This Cartesian theme is often repeated in other writings; for example, the preface to *The Protestant Doctrine of Freedom* encourages the reader 'not to take account of the age or novelty of beliefs, the number, titles or wealth of those who defend them, except as supports which are common to truth and error and, at most, as reasons for examining them'.[44] Before developing this idea a little more, a few remarks are necessary about the other source of misunderstanding, namely the Scriptures.

When *The Equality of the Sexes* was written it is clear that Poulain was already reconsidering the Catholic doctrine of the role of tradition and the Fathers of the Church, and perhaps even of an institutional church itself, in the interpretation of Scripture. In the Preface he suggests simply that Scripture 'has nothing to say on the question of equality', much as Galileo had argued earlier in the century that Scripture does not purport to teach astronomy. Therefore when people appeal to Scripture to defend the subjection of women, they are merely reading their own prejudices into a text which, in various ways, reflects the condition of women at the time in which it was written; Scripture is not attempting to teach that this condition is a matter of faith. When Poulain returns to the same question later in the text, in explaining how women could study theology, he claims that the various books of Scripture are 'no more difficult to understand than the Greek and Latin authors, and that those who read it [i.e. the New Testament] with childlike simplicity ... will discover its truth and meaning' (p. 96).

Almost forty-seven years later, what is only implicit in these remarks becomes explicit in *The Protestant Doctrine of Freedom*. Poulain considers three ways of interpreting Scripture: by relying on tradition, on the authoritative teaching of a church, or on reason. He argues against the first two approaches and endorses the third.

> Sound reason, good philosophy, criticism, are the genuine and natural interpreters of Holy Scripture ... Right reason also tells us: 1. to read the Holy Scripture at least in the same spirit and with the same attitude, and according to the same rules by which one reads and one ought to read all good books; 2. to examine

> and weigh up everything as if no one else had read or understood it before us.[45]

The reformer's understanding of how Scripture should be interpreted released Poulain from the traditional interpretation of Scripture, which suggested that women should be subject to men. The first fruits of this rejection of tradition are in Poulain's claim (p. 106) that women are just as capable as men of exercising the Christian ministry, a view which had all the hallmarks of a heresy in the seventeenth century.

Apart from scriptural or theological objections, Poulain invites readers to apply Descartes's method to the question of women's equality, and to reason the matter out for themselves. As already indicated above, Descartes challenged scholastic philosophers to go beyond how things appear to us and to hypothesise appropriate combinations of particles, described in terms of their primary qualities, in order to explain natural phenomena. Poulain adopts a similar strategy for the social phenomena relevant to women's condition. We cannot base our analysis on what he called 'superficial appearances' (p. 49), 'on the way things seem to be' (p. 53). We cannot justifiably argue that, because women are excluded from the positions of authority 'by which people usually measure perfection, . . . therefore, they are not as perfect as we are' (p. 78). This is the way school philosophers argue when they rely 'on judgements which they made since childhood . . . they consider it a crime or a mistake to cast doubt on' the spontaneous but misleading judgements which are based on uncritical observations (p. 84). Rather than follow this method which led them, for example, to believe mistakenly that the sun goes around the earth, we should go back to basics and begin with clear and distinct ideas (pp. 49, 46).

Since truth can only be reached by following a scientific method (p. 98), we have to approach the question about women's equality impartially and honestly. Secondly, we have to think clearly about it: 'one thinks properly when one applies one's mind seriously to the objects which present themselves, in order to get clear and distinct ideas of them, to consider them from every angle and in all their relations, and not to make any judgements about them except those which seem to be manifestly true' (pp. 91–2). In the present case, this includes considering what we know of the nature of men and women in terms of their souls and their bodies.

As regards the soul, it is axiomatic for Descartes that all human souls have the same nature; it follows that 'the mind has no sex' (p. 87), and that any sexual differences which are observed between men and women are exclusively a function of differences in their bodies. Not only has the mind no sex, but the mind works in the same way in men and women (p. 88), and is equal in all human beings (p. 87). In fact, Poulain repeats the Cartesian thesis that we all acquire naturally, without any effort on our part, the same store of 'natural' ideas (p. 85), and these occur in the same way in everyone, by the simple operation of our senses and our intellect. So if there are any differences in scientific knowledge between individuals, these differences must result from whether or not people have been trained to reflect on their ideas — as Poulain illustrates in the example of liquidity (p. 85) — or whether they have been impeded from doing so by the training of the schools.

The philosophy of the schools was described as corrupting the mind in a variety of ways. Apart from its tendency to endorse our unreflective common-sense opinions or prejudices, it filled the mind with vague, meaningless terms, usually in Latin, and gave the student the illusion of being much wiser than those who did not have the benefit of a similar education.[46] For example, scholastic philosophy attempted to explain natural phenomena by inventing mysterious faculties and powers, such as the 'digestive faculty' to explain digestion (p. 64); it became entangled in insoluble or meaningless questions, such as whether or not God could give exotic obediential powers to inanimate objects (p. 64). This kind of study was not only not helpful: it was a positive hindrance to genuine understanding. For this reason Poulain argued that women were lucky in so far as they were protected, as a result of men's prejudices, from the detrimental effects of such an education (p. 62). Indeed, the opinions about women which Aristotle, Plato and other illustrious philosophers were reputed to have held were such that it is difficult to disagree with Poulain's rhetorical claim that women are better off ignorant, if that is what counts as learning.

Assuming Poulain's Cartesian thesis that all minds are naturally equal and all receive ideas in the same way, it follows that women are just as capable as men of any intellectual enterprise on condition that their brains function as well as men's. Although seventeenth-century physiology was hardly advanced enough to answer this question, it is at least plausible for Poulain to argue that we must assume that women's brains are equal to men's as long as our anatomical investigations reveal no discernible differences between them. The prejudice is on the side of those who assume differences in women's brains, as Malebranche had, without providing any empirical evidence to support their contention. Not only women's brains, but all their other bodily organs apart from those directly involved in generation are equivalent to those of men. It follows from an examination of women's minds and bodies, therefore, that there is no reason to assume that women are naturally inferior to men, apart from obvious but irrelevant minor differences in physical strength between them.

This argument implies that women have exactly the same kind of mind or soul as men, and they also have the same kind of brain. Therefore they have the same innate capacities as men for any profession or civil office which does not presuppose brute strength. How then explain the patent inequalities which were observable in Poulain's day; how explain the social phenomena?

It is at this point that the hypotheses of the Cartesian tradition were put to work. Since we can find nothing in women's nature which could explain their inferior social roles, we have to look further afield and hypothesise a series of social factors, one compounding the other in the history of the sexes, which would adequately explain the current condition of women in society. This is the point of Poulain's historical hypothesis. It was irrelevant, in the Cartesian tradition, if this hypothesis was not an accurate picture of the development of societies; the purpose of the hypothesis was to suggest some conceivable way in which we can usefully imagine how women came to occupy such inferior roles in society despite their equality in relevant capacities with men. If anyone were to object that this hypothesis is unsatisfactory, then of course he would be challenged to provide an alternative account which corresponded with what we know of women's natural abilities.

In Poulain's hypothesis, custom and education hold the key to explaining women's condition. The only reason why people thought that women could not perform roles which were exclusively available to men was custom. If the position had been reversed, we would have believed with equal conviction that men could not possibly be priests, judges, rulers, etc. Once people's convictions became established, however it may have happened historically, they were reflected in educational practice. It was assumed that there was no reason to educate women for functions for which they lacked the natural capacities; thus the lack of access to education reinforced popular prejudices. For this reason, Poulain devoted a major portion of his argument to the benefits of women's education.

> If one finds that there is some fault or impediment in some women at present . . . that should be explained completely in terms of the external conditions of their sex and the education which they receive, which includes the ignorance in which they are left, the prejudices and errors which they are taught, . . . Is there anything in what women are taught which helps to give them a solid education? It seems on the contrary that their education has been designed to diminish their courage, obscure their minds, and . . . deprive them of any desire of improving themselves. (pp. 121, 123)

The detrimental effect of a spurious education (reserved for men) and the total lack of any worthwhile education for women was the theme of Poulain's *Dialogues on the Education of Women* (1674).

Poulain's treatise on education is distinctive from the first page of its preface in not proposing a special type of education for women. On the contrary he suggested that, since men and women are equal, his proposals concerning women's education apply equally to men.[47] Poulain's theory of education is borrowed from Descartes's philosophy: it includes a critique of current education and suggestions for a more successful alternative.

The critique of current education reflected the standard Cartesian assessment of the schools. Students learned by rote whatever their teachers taught; the teachers in turn borrowed from generally accepted, ancient authorities. 'While our reason was asleep, we made our memory work at taking in various things which could only be expressed in Latin.'[48] The only basis for accepting what was taught was the authority of the teachers, and the students accepted their authority by extending to teachers the child's belief in the authority of his parents.[49] In this way students learned to fill their heads with all kinds of uncritically accepted beliefs; 'they believed they knew a lot when in fact they knew nothing; their condition was worse than if they were completely ignorant of anything — in which case, having no idea of the truth, they would be less distant from it'.[50] It was in this sense that Poulain argued, in *The Equality of the Sexes*, that women are actually in a better position than men to study the various sciences because they do not have to begin by clearing their minds of counterfeit knowledge.

The alternative approach to study recommended by Poulain was to apply the methodic doubt of Descartes's *Meditations* and to accept as true only what is manifestly supported by appropriate evidence:

> To accept only what is true, to reject all beliefs which were accepted without examination and on the basis of other people's reports, to work as if one were alone in the conviction that one has an intellect and reason, with the aim of cultivating these faculties and following their lead in one's conduct.[51]

The age of a belief or theory is not an index of its truth, no more than its novelty implies that it is false.[52] Thus women can get no guidance about the truth of a theory from its age or its novelty, nor can they rely on the authority of teachers. They have nothing else to fall back on except their own native intelligence, their capacity for reasoning, and the ideas which spontaneously occur in the mind when it is not corrupted by false philosophy. Women are therefore already in a position to study all the sciences because they have those basic ideas on which all the sciences are based.[53] If they wish to be tutored by others, then Poulain recommends reading the following: Descartes's *Discourse on Method* and *Meditations*, the *Port Royal Logic*, Cordemoy's *Six Discourses on the Distinction and Union of Body and Mind*, Rohault's *Treatise on Physics*, Descartes's *Treatise on Man* together with the commentary by La Forge, and La Forge's own book on the nature of the mind.[54] It is obvious from this list that Poulain was not recommending an improved domestic science for women; he was proposing for women exactly the same kind of education which he would have chosen for men as an alternative to the established curriculum of the schools.

Having warned women (and men) of the dangers of joining a 'sect' and substituting blind faith for rational judgement, Poulain warns that one should read Descartes and the other Cartesian authors mentioned with the same kind of critical judgement required in reading any book.

> I beseech you to take care that I do not imagine here that Descartes is infallible, that everything he suggests is true or without difficulty, that one should follow him blindly, or that others may not discover something which is as good as, or even better than, what he has left us. I only say that he is one of the most reasonable philosophers we have, and that his method is the one which is most likely to help us discover the truth ourselves.[55]

This summary identifies those features of *The Equality of the Sexes* which were novel, or which were characteristic of the author as an exponent of Cartesian philosophy and its application to a major social debate of the seventeenth century. However it should also be kept in mind that there were dozens of participants in the same debate and that they often copied both the style and content of other contributors. Those who argued for the superiority of women invariably identified the same famous women to support their thesis; and although Poulain de la Barre was explicitly arguing for the equality of men and women, his paeans in praise of women are stylistically indistinguishable from Du Soucy's *Triumph of Women*, de Scudéry's *Illustrious Women*, or Gilbert's *Panegyric*. It is clear from the abundant literature on this issue in France in the seventeenth century that proponents of the women's cause were confronted by a rather narrow range of arguments against women; they were accused of lacking certain virtues (which men exemplified), and of suffering from certain character defects which were peculiar to their sex. In reply to these charges, it was customary to argue that women were no more lacking in virtue than men and to list many of the more virtuous women — in a 'gallery' of famous women — who were counter-examples to opponents' claims. Poulain's style of presentation is not novel in this respect; he appeals to famous cases of exemplary virtue in women, adopts the language of his most passionate supporters in praise of women's natural abilities and beauty, and follows the usual pattern of listing the many ways in which sensitive and 'polite' women are superior to uncouth, boorish and uneducated men.

Despite the similarity in style, however, with contemporary defenders of the women's cause, there is a radically new thesis camouflaged beneath the florid rhetoric of *The Equality of the Sexes*. This is the claim that men and women are essentially equal, that law and custom are not reliable guides to how we should decide the social roles of the sexes, that seventeenth-century France needed to revolutionise its educational system and make it available equally to men and women, and that there is no civil or ecclesiastical office for which women and men are not equally suited.

Poulain's treatise on the equality of the sexes was almost completely ignored in France in the seventeenth century. This was partly for reasons which he anticipated in the Preface. He feared that his book would be too casually accepted as belonging to a well-recognised genre of tracts in praise of women and, as already indicated, there is enough surface similarity between his contribution and that of many others to warrant such a misunderstanding. The second reason for his failure to make an impact on contemporaries was, possibly, that *The Equality of the Sexes* was so radical as to be unbelievable. Who would have believed, even in the reformed churches, that women could exercise the ministry or become professors of theology? In the period immediately following 1673, Cartesians were being censored and deprived of teaching posts in France, especially those who were thought to adopt dissident theological views. So the climate was hardly ripe for a Cartesian tract by a Huguenot ex-priest which went far beyond the set style of argumentation for and against the virtues of women.

The neglect of *The Equality of the Sexes* during Poulain's lifetime seems to have doomed the book to a corresponding oblivion after his death in Geneva. It achieved a temporary notoriety in the eighteenth century but soon afterwards faded back again into obscurity. When Henri Piéron found a copy in the Bibliothèque Nationale, Paris, at the beginning of the twentieth century, no one had ever opened it before.[56] The recent re-edition of the French text and a new English translation should help, in some way, to win for François Poulain de la Barre the place in the history of ideas which he deserves.

Notes to introduction

1 For example, apart from the articles cited in note 3 below, see Simone de Beauvoir, *Le deuxième sexe* (Paris: Gallimard, 1949), epigraph, and vol. I, 181; Michael A. Seidel, 'Poulain de la Barre's *The Woman as Good as the Man*', *Journal of the History of Ideas*, 35 (1974), 499–508; Carolyn C. Lougee, *Le Paradis des femmes: Women,*

Salons and Social Stratification in Seventeenth-century France (Princeton University Press, 1976), pp. 18–21; Michel Delon, 'Cartésanisme(s) et Féminisme(s)', *Europe*, No. 594 (October 1978), 73–86; M. Albistur and D. Armogathe, *Histoire du féminisme français du moyen âge à nos jours* (Paris: Editions des femmes, 1979), pp. 157–72; Claire Goldberg Moses, *French Feminism in the Nineteenth Century* (Albany: State University of New York Press, 1984), pp. 8–9; Joan Kelly, *Women, History and Theory* (Chicago and London: University of Chicago Press, 1984), pp. 75–6.

2 *The Woman as Good as the Man: Or, The Equallity of Both Sexes*. Written originally in French, and translated into English by A. L. (London: N. Brooks, 1677) (copy in the British Library).

3 Apart from some indications in Poulain's publications, the biographical information used here is borrowed from G. Lefèvre, 'Poulain de la Barre et le féminisme au xviie siècle', *Revue Pédagogique*, 64 (1914), 101–13; H. Grappin, 'Notes sur un féministe oublié: le cartésien Poullain de la Barre', *Revue d'histoire littéraire de la France* (1913), 852–67, and 'A propos du féministe Poullain de la Barre', *Revue d'histoire littéraire de la France* (1914), 387–9.

4 For a detailed discussion of education in France in this period, see L. W. D. Brockliss, *French Higher Education in the Seventeenth and Eighteenth Centuries* (Oxford: Clarendon Press, 1987).

5 *Ibid.*, pp. 332, 333.

6 *De l'éducation des dames pour la conduite de l'esprit, dans les sciences et dans les moeurs: Entretiens* (Paris: Jean du Puis, 1674), pp. 332–3. (Note: the date of publication is incorrectly given on the title page as 1671, whereas the correct date is given at the end of the book.) Poulain continued to argue against the utility of studying Latin. In the preface to his book on French grammar, he decries the time spent on teaching Latin rather than French or some other living language, while *La doctrine des Protestans* is a defence of the use of the vernacular in the liturgy, in reading the Scriptures and in the invocation of the saints.

7 The author of the *The Equality of the Sexes* was identified in the text only as Sieur P. and, as late as 1685, the *Nouvelles de la République des Lettres* speculated incorrectly about the identity of the author. See Grappin, 'Notes sur un féministe oublié', p. 867. The apparent problem in identifying the author is difficult to reconcile with the fact that the name 'Poulain' appears at the conclusion of the dedication to his *Dialogues on the Education of Women* (1674), in which he twice refers to the author of the book about the equality of the sexes (pp. 2, 55).

8 *De l'excellence des hommes, contre l'égalite des sexes* (Paris: Jean du Puis, 1675), preface, p. 4. The first edition contained a lengthy preface, together with the main text divided into two parts. When reprinted in 1692 together with *The Equality of the Sexes*, the new volume included an apparently new third part, entitled: *Dissertation ou Discours, pour servir de Troisiéme Partie au Livre de l'Egalité des deux Sexes, et de répondre aux authorités de l'Ecriture Sainte, qu'on rapporte dans la Seconde Partie du Traitté de l'Excellence des Hommes, contre l'Egalité des deux Sexes* (Paris: Jean du Puis, 1692). The apparently new third part is in fact the preface of the first edition (beginning on the second page) transposed to a new, more logical position for a single-volume edition of Poulain's writings on sexual equality. This new edition includes: 1. *The Equality of the Sexes*; 2. *The Superiority of Men*, a statement of the opposite view which relies significantly on arguments from Scripture; and 3. The Preface of *The Superiority of Men*, which answers the scriptural arguments in favour of men's superiority which had been canvassed in part 2. Pierre Bayle, *Dictionnaire historique et critique*, 4 vols., 5th ed. (Amsterdam, Leiden, Hague and Utrecht: 1740), acknowledges the apparent oddity of the title of *De l'excellence des hommes,* when he mentions Poulain's work in a footnote to an entry on Lucrece Marinella (vol. III, 334).

9 *La Doctrine des protestans sur la liberté de lire l'Ecriture Sainte, le service divin en langue entendue, l'invocation des saints, le sacrement de l'eucharistie. Justifiée par le Missel Romain & par des Réfléxions sur chaque*

point. Avec un commentaire philosophique sur ces paroles de Jesus-Christ, Ceci est mon Corps; Ceci est mon Sang, Matth. Chap. XXVI, v. 26 (Geneva: Fabri & Barrillot, 1720).

10 *Essai des remarques particulieres sur la langue françoise, pour la ville de Geneve* (Geneva: 1691). There is no author's name on the title page; however, the dedication to Madame Perdriau concludes with the name: De La Barre.

11 Louis de la Forge, *l'Homme de René Descartes et un Traité de la Formation du Foetus du mesme autheur. Avec les Remarques de Louis de la Forge* (Paris, 1664); Louis de la Forge, *Traité de l'Esprit de l'Homme* (Paris, 1666).

12 For a more comprehensive discussion of Cartesianism in France in the period after 1660, see D. Clarke, *Occult Powers and Hypotheses: Cartesian Natural Philosophy under Louis* XIV (Oxford: Clarendon Press, 1989).

13 Descartes's philosophical works were condemned on 20 November 1663; Malebranche's *Treatise on Nature and Grace* (1680) was put on the Index in 1690.

14 *De l'éducation des dames*, unpaginated preface.

15 Nicolas Malebranche, *Recherche de la vérité*, vol. 1 of *Oeuvres*, ed. G. Rodis-Lewis (Paris: Vrin, 1972), pp. 266–8; *The Search after Truth, and Elucidations of the Search after Truth*, trans. T. M. Lennon and P. J. Olscamp (Columbus, Ohio: Ohio State University Press, 1980), pp. 130–1. In comparing the imagination of men and women, Malebranche argues that

> the delicacy of the brain fibers is one of the principal causes impeding our efforts to apply ourselves to discovering truths that are slightly hidden. This delicacy of the brain fibers is usually found in women, and this is what gives them great understanding of everything that strikes the senses. It is for women to set fashions, judge language, discern elegance and good manners. They have more knowledge, skill, and finesse than men in these matters. Everything that depends upon taste is within their area of competence, but normally they are incapable of penetrating to truths that are slightly dif-

> ficult to discover. Everything abstract is incomprehensible to them. They cannot use their imagination for working out complex and tangled questions. They consider only the surface of things, ... A trifle is enough to distract them, the slightest cry frightens them, the least motion fascinates them. (p. 130)

Malebranche goes on to admit that this is true generally of women, though not necessarily of every individual woman. However, 'the fibers of most women's brains ... remain extremely delicate throughout their lives. ... Suffice it to say of women and children that since they are not involved in seeking truth and teaching others, their errors do not cause much prejudice, for one hardly takes their proposals seriously' (p. 131). Having disposed of women because of the infirmity of their brains, Malebranche continues: 'Let us speak of grown men, whose minds are strong and vigorous ...' (p. 131). It is evident that, for Malebranche, the difference in intellectual ability which he assumes between most women and men is a function of physiological differences in their brains rather than in their souls.

16 For a recent discussion of feminism in French literature in the period immediately preceding Poulain's *Equality of the Sexes*, see Ian Maclean, *Women Triumphant: Feminism in French Literature 1610–1652* (Oxford: Clarendon Press, 1977); for a more general survey, see M. Albistur and D. Armogathe, *Histoire du féminisme français* (note 1 above).

17 Desiderius Erasmus, *Opera Omnia* (Leiden: Peter Vander, 1706), Vol. IV, *Stultitiae Laus*, p. 418; *The Praise of Folly*, trans. with an introduction and commentary by Clarence H. Miller (New Haven and London: Yale University Press, 1979), pp. 28–9. This text from Erasmus was subsequently used widely as a gloss on Plato, although the original text to which it refers, *Timaeus* 91 A–D, does not support Erasmus's interpretation.

18 See for example E. W. Monter, *Witchcraft in France and Switzerland: The Borderlands during the Reformation* (Ithaca and London: Cornell University Press, 1976).

19 Jacques Olivier, *Alphabet de l'imperfection et*

malice des femmes (Paris: Antoine Ferrand, 1617), pp. 3–4.

20 Le Sieur Vigoureux, *La defense des femmes, contre l'Alphabet de leur pretendue malice & imperfection* (Paris: Pierre Chevalier, 1617). Vigoureux argues that Plato did not mean what authors generally understood him to claim about the status of women (see note 17 above); Plato should be interpreted as saying that, despite the fact that men and women are equally rational, one might wonder if women were genuinely rational because of the way in which they have been mistreated (pp. 22–3).

21 J. Olivier, *Responce aux impertinences de l'aposté capitaine Vigoureux: sur la defence des femmes* (Paris: Jean Petit-Pas, 1617), p. 29.

22 *Ibid.*, pp. 45, 100.

23 *Ibid.*, p. 30. Rolet, *Tableau historique* (see following note), is explicit that women are the source of all evil in the world: 'I have always noticed, with one of the great philosophers of antiquity, that there is no animal in the world more dangerous than woman. . . . I believe that she is the exclusive nursery and source of all the evils which have inundated the world' (pp. 3–4).

24 L.S.R. [i.e Rolet], *Tableau historique des ruses et subtilitez des femmes* (Paris: Rolet Boutonne, 1623), p. 86. Rolet claims that, since the malice of women tends to infinity, he would run short of paper if he were to give a complete account of his subject from the beginning of the world.

25 François Du Soucy, Sieur de Gerzan, *Le Triomphe des Dames* (Paris: chez l'autheur, 1646); J. Guillaume, *Les dames illustres ou par bonnes et fortes raisons, il se prouve, que le Sexe feminin surpasse en toutes sortes de genres le Sexe masculin* (Paris: Thomas Jolly, 1665).

26 G. Gilbert, *Panegyrique des Dames* (Paris: Augustin Courbé, 1650) pp. 4–6, 13–14.

27 *Le Triomphe des Dames*, pp. 199–201, 214. The argument from God's creation had been used in a similar way by Jacquette Guillaume, *Les dames illustres*, p. 12:

> God . . . first made the land and the sea, then plants and fish, and other animals. Then he created man as

> the master of all these things, and finally he created woman, as the masterpiece of nature, and the model of all perfections: mistress of man, stronger than him as Scripture informs us, and therefore mistress of all creatures.

28 [Père Du Bosc], *L'Honneste Femme* (Paris: Pierre Billaine, 1632); François de Grenaille, *L'Honneste fille* (Paris: J. Paslé, 1639–40).

29 Moyse Amyraut, *Considerations sur les droits par lesquels la nature a reiglé les marriages* (Saumur: Isaac Desbordes, 1648). Amyraut is concerned primarily with providing a natural law argument against bigamy, polyandry, etc.; in general, in favour of the marriage practices of the day. In the course of his argument he seems to assume that wives are not equal to their husbands, for example at p. 173.

30 Père Pierre le Moyne, *La Gallerie des Femmes fortes* (Paris: Antoine de Sommaville, 1647), pp. 10, 154.

31 Louis Machon, *Discours ou Sermon apologetique, en faveur des femmes. Question nouvelle, curieuse, & non jamais soustenue* (Paris: T. Blaise, 1641); George de Scudery, *Les femmes illustres, ou les harangues heroiques de Monsieur de Scudery, avec les veritables portraits de ces Heroines, tirez des Medailles Antiques* (Paris: Antoine de Sommaville & A. Courbé, 1642). The latter was written by Madeleine de Scudery, but published under the name of her brother, George.

32 Mario Schiff, *La Fille d'alliance de Montaigne, Marie de Gournay* (Paris: Champion, 1910), includes *Egalité des hommes et des femmes* (pp. 57–77), and *Le grief des dames* (pp. 89–97). In the last paragraph of the book Marie de Gournay explains that she avoids the extreme views of those who defend the superiority of women: 'I am content to make them (i.e women) equal with men' (p. 61).

33 Marie de Gournay, *Egalité des hommes et des femmes* (Schiff ed.), p. 70.

34 Du Soucy, *Le Triomphe des Dames*, pp. 107–8.

35 Du Bosc, *L'Honneste Femme*, p. 188.

36 Louis de Lesclache, *Les Avantages que les femmes peuvent recevoir de la Philosophie, et principalement de la*

Morale; ou l'abregé de cette science (Paris: Laurent Rondet, 1667), pp. 173, 174. De Lesclache operated a very successful school for a number of years and provided a summary of philosophy for his pupils in a five-part *Cours de philosophie* (1650–52); however, he lost most of his clients to the new philosophy and his lack of enthusiasm for his successful competitors is obvious in the way he describes the vanity of scientific experiments.

37 *Question celebre. S'il est necessaire, ou non, que les Filles soient sçavantes. Agitée de part & d'autre, par Mademoiselle Anne Marie de Schurman Holandoise, & le Sr. André Rivet Poitevin* (Paris: Rolet le Duc, 1646). The general argument on Schurman's side was that women need knowledge as much as men in order to live properly and to distinguish good and evil.

38 I am indebted to C. Lougee's book (see note 1 above), especially Chapters XI and XII (pp. 173–95), for the next few paragraphs. I quote Fénelon's text from H. C. Barnard, *Fénelon on Education* (Cambridge University Press, 1966), which includes a translation of the full text of the *Traité de l'éducation des filles*.

39 *The Education of Girls*, pp. 1–2.

40 *Ibid.*, p. 75.

41 *Ibid.*, pp. 65–74.

42 Desiderius Erasmus, *On the Education of Children*, trans. and ed. Beert C. Verstraete, in *Collected Works of Erasmus* (London and Toronto: University of Toronto Press, 1985), vol. 26, p. 325. The original title was: *De pueris statim ac liberaliter instituendis declamatio*, which is obviously about the education of *boys*.

43 *Six Books of the Commonwealth*, abridged and translated by M. J. Tooley (Oxford: Blackwell, 1967), p. 203. The original text is found in *Les Six Livres de la République* (1576) (Paris: Fayard, 1986), VI, pp. 232–3. Bodin supports his claim about the law of God by reference to *Genesis* 3:16 where God said to Eve that 'thy desire shall be to thy husband, and he shall rule over thee'.

44 *La doctrine des Protestans*, pp. xi–xii of the Preface.

45 *Ibid.*, pp. 267, 274–5. The implications for women of this approach to scripture are worked out in detail in the Preface to *De l'excellence des hommes.*

46 The standard objection to scholastic philosophy is more directly expressed in *La doctrine des Protestans*, p. 143: 'Scholastic philosophy which loves occult qualities offers mysterious and inconceivable powers instead of simple and natural causes, and it attributes to external objects qualities which are similar to the impressions which they cause in us, to the sensations which they excite in us.'

47 *De l'éducation des dames*, p. 1 of the unpaginated *Avertissement.*

48 *Ibid.*, p. 88.

49 *Ibid.*, pp. 66–7.

50 *Ibid.*, p. 66.

51 *Ibid.*, p. 148.

52 *Ibid.*, p. 182.

53 *Ibid.*, p. 214.

54 Antoine Arnauld and Pierre Nicole, *La Logique ou l'art de penser* (Paris, 1662); Gerauld de Cordemoy, *Le discernement du Corps et de l'Ame* (Paris, 1666); Jacques Rohault, *Traité de Physique* (Paris, 1671); the two books by La Forge are listed in note 11 above.

55 *De l'éducation des dames*, p. 325. Cf. the same advice from Malebranche for readers of his *Search after Truth*, on p. 215:

> Descartes was a man among men, and like men, subject to error and illusion; there is not one of his works including even his Geometry, that does not bear the mark of the human mind's weakness. He should not be believed on his word, then, but should be read as he himself warns us — with great care, examining whether he has not made a mistake, and believing nothing he says until obliged to do so by evidence and the secret reproaches of our reason.

56 H. Grappin, 'Notes sur un féministe oublié', p. 852.

A Physical and Moral Discourse on the Equality of the Sexes, which shows the importance of getting rid of one's prejudices

1673

Table of Contents

Preface

The strongest objections which can be made against us derive from the authority of famous men, and from Holy Scripture. As regards the first of these, I think that I can answer them satisfactorily by saying that I recognise no authority apart from the authority of reason and of sound judgement. As far as Scripture is concerned, it is not in any way contrary to the aim of this work, as long as one understands each of them correctly. I claim here that the two sexes are completely equal, once they are considered independently of custom which often makes those who have more intelligence and merit subordinate to others who have less. Scripture says nothing about inequality; since its only function is to provide a rule of conduct for people in accordance with the ideas of justice which it provides, it leaves everyone free to judge as they wish about the natural and true state of things. If one keeps that in mind, all the objections which are derived from Scripture are only the fallacious arguments of prejudice, by which some passages are understood as if they applied to all women when they refer only to some individuals in particular, or something is attributed to nature which results only from education or custom or from what the sacred authors say about the customs of their own time.

Introduction
Containing the plan and purpose of this Discourse

There is nothing more delicate than the challenge of explaining one's views about women. When a man speaks in their favour, people think immediately that he does so for reasons of gallantry or love. There is a great danger that the majority of readers, judging this book by its title, will think right away that it results from either gallantry or love and they will assume that they know its real purpose and aim, which are as follows.

The most propitious thought which can occur to those who try to acquire well-founded knowledge, when they have been instructed according to the usual methods, is to doubt if they have learned anything properly and to wish to discover the truth themselves. In the course of their search for truth, they inevitably notice that we are filled with prejudices* and that it is necessary to give these up completely in order to have clear and distinct understanding.

In the hope of persuading readers of such an important maxim, I thought it was best to choose a specific, striking issue which is interesting to everyone. Thus, once I have shown that an opinion as old as the world and as universal as the human race is a prejudice or a mistake, the learned may be convinced eventually of the need to judge things for themselves after they have examined them thoroughly and, if they wish to avoid mistakes, not to

* That is to say, judgements which are made about things without examining them.

defer to the opinion or sincerity of others. Of all the prejudices available, no one has found a more appropriate choice for this purpose than the prejudice which is commonly held about the inequality of the two sexes.

In fact, if one considers the two sexes in their current condition, one finds that they are less equal in their civil roles and in those things which depend on using one's mind than in things which pertain to the body. If one looks for an explanation of this in the standard treatises, one finds that everyone agrees — those who have studied and those who have not, and even women themselves — in saying that women have no part in the sciences and employment because they are not capable of having any, that they have less intelligence than men, and that they ought to be inferior to men in everything just as they are.

Criterion of truth

When I examined this opinion according to the criterion of truth, which is: not to accept anything as true which is not based on clear and distinct ideas, two things became clear; on the one hand, it is false and based on prejudice and popular tradition. On the other hand, it was found that the two sexes are equal, that is, that women are as noble, as perfect and as capable as men. This claim can be established only by refuting two kinds of opponents: the common or untutored, and almost all the learned.

Since the first kind of opponent has no basis for his belief apart from custom and superficial appearances, it seems as if the best way of combating him is to get him to see how women have been dominated and excluded from the sciences and from employment. Having guided him through the principal stages and important occasions of life, he can be given an opportunity of seeing that women have advantages which make them equal to men. This comprises the first part of this treatise.

The second part is designed to show that the arguments of the learned are all vain. Once I establish the thesis about equality by means of positive arguments, I subsequently exonerate women of the faults of which they are usually accused by showing that they are either imagined or insignificant, that they derive exclusively from the education which they are given and that they point to significant ways in which women are superior.

This issue about equality can be discussed in two ways: either in a gallant fashion, that is in a flowery and playful style, or philosophically and by reference to principles, so that one understands it thoroughly.

Those who have an accurate idea of genuine eloquence realise that these two ways are almost incompatible, and that one can rarely enlighten the mind and entertain it at the same time. It is not as if one could not combine flowery speech with reason; it is rather that such a combination often hinders achieving the objective which one should have for discourses, namely to convince and persuade. When something pleasant entertains the mind, it prevents it from concentrating on substantive issues.

People look on women from their own point of view. Thus, if one includes some element of gallantry in a book about women, those who read it let their thoughts run too far afield and lose sight of what they ought to be concerned with. For that reason, since there is nothing of greater concern to women than this project — in which one ought to say what is most convincing and true in their defence, in so far as a frivolous world will tolerate it — I thought it was necessary to speak seriously and to warn readers of this; I was afraid that any suggestion that this might be simply a book in praise of women would either make it too easily acceptable or else cause it to be rejected by careful readers.

I am not unaware of the fact that this discourse will make many people unhappy, and that those whose interests or maxims are opposed to what is suggested here will not miss an opportunity for objecting to it. In order to provide a way of answering their objections I warn intelligent people, especially women who are not duped by those who are in authority over them, that if they take the trouble to read this treatise carefully — which the very diversity of issues involved requires — they will notice that the essential mark of truth is clarity and evidence. This will enable people to decide if the objections which they encounter are serious or not. They will be able to notice that the most specious objections will be made by people whose profession seems to commit them at present to rejecting experience, sound judgement and even themselves, in order to accept blindly whatever agrees with their prejudices and their interests and to fight against all kinds of truths which appear to challenge them.

I hope people will consider that the harmful consequences which panic makes them fear in this undertaking may never affect even one woman, and that these effects will be counterbalanced by the great benefits which women may gain. Perhaps there is no more natural or more sure way of rescuing women from the idleness to which they have been reduced and from its harmful effects than to encourage them to study — almost the only thing to which women can nowadays devote themselves — by getting them to realise that they are as well suited to it as men.

Just as it is only unreasonable men who abuse the advantages which custom confers on them to the detriment of women, so also it could only be women of poor judgement who would use this work to rebel against those men who would treat them as their equals and their companions. Finally, if anyone is shocked by this discourse for whatever reason, let him blame the truth and not the author. To alleviate his chagrin he might tell himself that it is only an intellectual game; it is certain that such a trick of the imagination, or something similar which prevents the truth from taking hold of us, will make the truth much less troublesome for those who have difficulty in accepting it.

Part I

In which the common belief is shown to be a prejudice and that, by comparing impartially what can be observed in the conduct of men and women, one is forced to recognise a complete equality between the two sexes.

Men are convinced of many things which they cannot explain, because their conviction is based only on superficial appearances, by which they have allowed themselves to be carried away. They would have believed the opposite just as strongly, if the impressions they get from their senses or from custom had persuaded them of it in a similar way.

Men are full of prejudices

Apart from a small number of learned people everyone thinks that it is an indubitable truth that the sun moves around the earth, despite the fact that what we know of the revolution of the days and the years leads those who examine it to believe that it is the earth which moves around the sun.[1] People imagine — by the same reasoning by which savages suppose that there is a little demon inside clocks and machines which they are shown, when they are not aware of their inner springs nor of how they are made — that animals have some kind of knowledge which guides them.[2]

If someone had reared us in the middle of the sea so that we never got close to land, we would surely have believed — as children do in a boat leaving a port — that it is the shoreline which moves relative to us when we move about in a boat. Everyone imagines that his own country is the best because he is more accustomed to it than others, and that the religion in which he was reared is the true religion which must be followed, even if he never thought of examining it or comparing it with others. One always finds oneself more inclined towards fellow countrymen than towards foreigners, even in cases where the law favours the latter. We get on better with members of our own profession even if they are less intelligent or virtuous than others. Inequalities in property and circumstances make many believe that men are not equal to each other.

If one examines the basis of all these diverse beliefs, one finds that they are based only on interest or on custom. One also finds that it is incomparably more difficult to get people to change their minds about something if their views are based only on prejudice than when they have adopted their views for reasons which seemed to be convincing and reliable.

One could add to these beliefs [based on prejudice] the common belief in the difference between the sexes, and especially everything which follows from this belief. There is no belief more ancient or widespread. Both the learned and the ignorant are so biased in believing that women are inferior to men in ability and in what they deserve, and that women should be dependents as we see them in our own time, that they will surely consider the contrary opinion as an odd paradox.*

What needs to be done to decide issues properly

Nevertheless, it would not be necessary to use any positive reasons to establish this paradoxical belief if men were more impartial and less biased in their judgements. It would be enough to warn them that, up to now, people have talked only superficially of the difference between the sexes, to the disadvantage of women. In order to decide judiciously if our sex has a natural superiority over women, we would have to consider the matter seriously and without bias, rejecting anything we accepted merely on the basis of someone else's report when we had not investigated the matter ourselves.

It is certain that any man who assumed this attitude of impartiality and distinterest would realise that, on the one hand, it is a lack of understanding and undue haste which makes us believe that women are less noble or less excellent than us men and that it is some natural

* An opinion which is contrary to what is commonly believed.

indispositions which make women subject to the faults or imperfections which are attributed to them and which make them, as a result, despised by so many people. On the other hand he would see that even those appearances, which deceive people about this issue when they consider them only superficially, can be used to correct him if he examines them even a little in greater depth. Finally, if this man were a philosopher,[3] he would find that there are physical explanations which prove indubitably that the two sexes are equal both in body and mind.

However, since there are not many individuals who are in a position to implement this kind of advice on their own, it would remain useless advice unless one took the trouble to work with them and help them to implement it. Because the beliefs of those who have not studied are the most widespread, it is necessary to begin our examination with their views.

What men believe about women

If one asks each man individually what he thinks generally of women and if he is willing to speak sincerely, he will surely say that women are created only for us and that they are hardly suited to anything more than raising young children and taking care of the home. Perhaps the more perceptive will add that there are many women of understanding and good conduct. However, they would add that if we examined more closely those who best exemplify these traits, one would always find something which betrays their sex; for example, that women do not have the steadfastness, control or depth of understanding that people imagined they had, and that it is as a result of divine providence and the wisdom of men that women are barred from the sciences, from government and from employment; that it would be amusing to see a woman lecturing on rhetoric or medicine from a chair, as professors do, marching on the streets followed by the commissioners and sergeants to enforce the law, pleading before a judge as a lawyer, sitting in a tribunal delivering justice at the head of a court, leading an army and engaging in battle, or addressing commonwealths or princes as head of a diplomatic mission.

I agree that this would surprise us, but that would be

only because of its novelty. In creating the various offices of the realm and in establishing the various functions which they exercise, if we had invited women to participate in them, we would be just as accustomed to seeing them in these roles now as they are accustomed to seeing us in them; and we would not find it any more unusual to see them sitting as judges on the bench than seeing them in the shops.[4]

If people are pressed a little more on this question, one finds that their strongest reasons come down to saying that, as far as women are concerned, things have always been the way they are at present; that this is a sign that they should be that way and that, if women had been capable of study and of holding civil offices, men would have admitted them before now.

The false idea of custom

These arguments derive from whatever opinion one holds about men's fairness, and from a mistaken understanding of custom. It is enough to find a custom established to believe that it is well founded. Since it is believed that men should never act unreasonably, most people cannot imagine that reason was ignored in the introduction of practices which they see so universally accepted; people assume that it was reason and prudence which initiated such practices because both reason and prudence force us to respect them as long as one cannot avoid following them without getting into trouble.

Why it is believed that women are inferior to men

Everyone sees in his own country women who are so dominated that they are dependent on men for everything; they are excluded from the sciences, and from any of the professions which provide an opportunity for distinguishing oneself by one's intellectual abilities. No one reports observing anything else in the condition of women. It is also known that things have always been that way, and that there is no place on earth where women are not treated as they are in those places where we live ourselves. There are even places where women are regarded as slaves. In China, their feet are bound up from infancy to prevent women leaving their houses, where they hardly ever see anyone except their husbands and their children. In Turkey, women are just as rigidly constrained. They are not much better off in Italy. Almost all the peoples of Asia, Africa, and America use women as they use servants here in France. Everywhere they work only at jobs which are considered menial; and since they are the only ones who look after the trivial concerns of the household and of children, people are generally convinced that women are in the world for that reason alone and that they are incapable of anything else. People have great difficulty in imagining how things could be much different; it seems as if one could never change anything, no matter how hard one tried.

The most wise legislators, in founding their commonwealths, have done nothing to benefit women in this respect. All laws seem to have been designed just to maintain men in possession of what they already have. Almost all those who were considered learned and who said anything about women, said nothing in their favour. One finds the behaviour of men so uniform in this respect, in every age and all over the world, that it seems as if they have conspired together or, as some imagine, that they have been driven to some such agreement by a hidden instinct, i.e. by a general commandment of the Author of nature.

One becomes more convinced of this if one considers the way in which women themselves tolerate their condition. They regard it as natural for themselves, either because they do not think about what they are, or because they think about it in the same way as men as a result of being born and growing up in a dependent condition. On all these issues, both men and women believe that women's minds are as different from men's as their bodies, and that there should be as much difference between the sexes in all areas of life as there is in those which are peculiar to each sex. However this belief, just like most of those which we hold about customs and practices, is a complete prejudice which we base on the way things seem to be, because we have failed to examine them more closely. We would correct this prejudice if we bothered to get to its sources and to judge in many cases about what happened in earlier times by reference to what

How to evaluate ancient customs

happens today, and to make up our minds about ancient customs by reference to those which we see develop in our own time. If we followed that rule, we would not have made so many mistakes in a great number of judgements. As regards the current condition of women, it would have been recognised that they were dominated only by the law of the strongest, and that it was not because of a lack of natural ability or merit that they have not shared with us in whatever raises our sex above theirs.

How people have always been governed

Indeed when one examines human affairs candidly, in the past and in the present, one finds that they are all the same on one point, namely, that reason has always been at its weakest. It seems as if all histories have been devised only in order to illustrate what each person sees during his own time, namely, that as long as men have existed, force has always prevailed. The greatest empires of Asia were, from the beginning, the creation of usurpers and thieves; and the remnants of the Greek and Roman empires were inherited only by those who thought they were strong enough to resist their rulers and dominate those who were their equals. This kind of conduct is equally apparent in every society. If men used that strategy in relation to their equals, there is every likelihood that each of them first acted in the same way, with even greater reason, in relation to his wife. Here is more or less how it happened.

Historical conjecture

How men put themselves in charge

Men noticed that they were stronger and, in relations between the sexes, they realised that they had an advantage in physical strength. They concluded, therefore, that they had a similar advantage over women in everything. The consequences were not too significant for women at the beginning of the world. Things were very different then from the way they are today, because there was no government, science, employment, or an established religion at that time. Besides, the ideas of dependence were in no way disagreeable. I imagine that men were like children, that any advantages they had were more like those one finds in a child's game; both men and women were simple and innocent then, and they spent their time equally on the cultivation of the earth or in hunting just as savages do still.[5] Men participated in their way and so likewise did women; whoever did best was most esteemed by all the others.

The inconveniences of pregnancy and its consequences diminished the strength of women for periods of time and hindered them from working as they had before, so that the help of their husbands became absolutely necessary, and even more so when they had children. This resulted in nothing more than a few signs of esteem or preference as long as families were composed only of a father and mother, together with a few small children. However, once the families became enlarged — when the father and his mother, grandchildren, brothers and sisters, the old and the young, were in the same house together — at that stage dependence increased and became more noticeable. One could see the mistress of the house submit to her husband, the son honour the father, and the father with authority over his children. And since it is very difficult for brothers to live in perfect harmony, one can infer that they were only a short time together when difficulties emerged between them. The strongest of the oldest ones was unwilling to concede anything to the others; sheer strength obliged the smaller ones to submit to those who were bigger. The girls followed the example of their mother.

It is easy to imagine that there were different roles in such houses. Since women were forced to remain at home to raise their children they took care of the home while the men, who were more free and robust, took care of things outside the home. After the death of the father and mother, the oldest son wanted to dominate the family. Since the girls were used to remaining at home, they did not even consider leaving it. A few of the younger children who were dissatisfied and more fearless than the others refused to submit, and were forced to retreat and start a new family. A few like-minded ones met and discussed their common lot and became friends easily; seeing themselves completely without any property, they looked for ways of acquiring some. Since there was no way of doing this except by taking some from others, they seized whatever property was nearest to them and, in order to protect their new acquisitions, they also seized the proprietor to whom the goods belonged.

The voluntary dependence which obtained in families ceased as a result of this invasion. Fathers and mothers, together with their children, were forced to obey an unjust usurper; the condition of women became even more burdensome than before. Instead of marrying members of their own family who would treat them like sisters, as they had up to then, they were forced to accept as husbands unknown outsiders who thought of them only as the best looking of their spoils.

Why women did not get a share of the first employments

It is customary for victors to despise those among the conquered whom they regard as the weakest. Since women seemed to be such, because their roles required less strength than men, they were considered to be inferior to men.

Some men were content with this first stage of their domination. However others were more ambitious and, encouraged by the success of their victory, wished to extend their conquests. Women were too gentle to participate in their unjust plans and were left at home; by contrast, men were chosen as being more suitable for undertakings in which strength was required. In this situation, things were valued only to the extent that they were thought to be useful for realising some goal; since the desire to dominate others became one of the strongest passions and it could only be satisfied by violence and injustice, it is not surprising that because men were exclusively the instruments of domination, they were preferred to women. They were used to consolidate the conquests which had been made; they were the only ones consulted in imposing tyranny because they alone were able to implement it and in this way the gentleness and kindness of women was the reason why they had no share in the government of states.

The example of princes was soon imitated by their subjects. Everyone wanted to get the better of his neighbour. Individuals began to dominate their families even more completely. When a lord found himself in charge of a people and a reasonably big region, he turned it into a kingdom. He made laws to govern it, chose officers from among the men, and put in command those who had served him best in his undertakings. Such a strong preference for one sex over the other resulted in the women being even less esteemed than before; since they were far removed from war and carnage by their natural disposition and their duties, they were considered to be incapable of contributing to the protection of kingdoms except by helping to populate them.

The establishment of states could not be realised without making distinctions among those who composed them. Marks of honour were introduced which helped to distinguish people; and signs of respect were invented to indicate the distinctions which were recognised between different people. In that way, the idea of power was linked with the public submission which one shows to those who hold authority.

How women failed to share in the ministry of pagan religions

It is not necessary to explain here how God became known to men. However, he has been adored in an uninterrupted way from the beginning of the world. As regards the worship which was rendered to God, it was only regularised when people gathered together in commonwealths. Since people were accustomed to honouring the powerful by marks of respect, it was thought that God should be honoured by some ceremonies which would help to express the feelings people had about his greatness. Temples were built, sacrifices were instituted, and the men who were already in charge of governing did not fail once again to monopolise everything to do with Religion. Since custom had already forewarned women that everything belongs to men, they did not request any part in the ministry. The idea people had of God was very much corrupted by fables and poetic fictions, so they constructed male and female divinities and established priestesses for serving the gods of their own sex; this however was only tolerated under the control and at the pleasure of the priests.

At times women have also been seen governing large states; but one need not assume for that reason that they had been called to this out of a spirit of restitution. They had so much skill in management that no one could take away this authority from them. Today there are hereditary states in which women succeed men, as queens or princesses; but there is reason to believe that if those kingdoms were originally allowed to be ruled by women, it was only in order to avoid a civil war. And if regencies were tolerated, it was only done in the belief that mothers, who always had such an extraordinary love of their children, would take special care of the states during their children's minority.

Why women had no part in the sciences

Thus women had only housework to do and, because they found that they had enough in that to keep them busy, it is not surprising that they discovered no sciences, the majority of which initially were only the work and occupation of the idle and the lazy. The Egyptian priests who had little to do amused themselves by talking together about those natural phenomena which affected them the most. By using their reason, they made observations the fame of which excited the curiosity of some men who came in search of them. Because the sciences were only in their infancy at that time, they did not entice women out of their houses; besides, the jealousy which already disturbed their husbands would have made them believe that the women visited the priests more for the love of their person than for the knowledge which they possessed.

When some men became imbued with knowledge, they gathered together in various places to talk about it at their leisure. With everyone expressing their ideas, the sciences developed. Academies were founded to which women were not invited, and in this way they were excluded from the sciences just as they had been excluded from everything else.

The constraints within which they were kept did not prevent some of them from having conversations with the learned and reading their works. In a short time they became equal to the most accomplished; since women were already burdenend by the demands of propriety men did not dare join them, nor did other women because they were afraid that others might be offended by it. As a result, women did not make any disciples or followers and everything they had learned died with them.

If one considers how fashions are introduced and how they develop from one day to the next one can easily see that, at the beginning of the world, there was little concern with fashion. Everything was simple and crude. People were concerned only about necessities. People skinned animals and made clothes for themselves by joining the skins together. Fashion came later; everyone dressed in his own style, and the best styles flourished. Those who were subject to the same prince did not fail to follow his example.

Why women became involved in trivialities

In the case of fashions, things were not the same as in the case of government and the sciences. Women took part in them together with men; when men noticed that women were better at fashions, they made sure not to deprive them of them. Both sexes found that they had more grace and were more pleasing in certain clothes, and they vied with each other in designing them. However, since men's occupations were more important and prestigious, they were prevented from concerning themselves with fashion as much as women.

Women showed their prudence and their skill in this. Once they noticed that artificial decorations made men look on them with more gentleness and that this in turn made their own condition more tolerable, they neglected nothing which they thought might help to make them more attractive. That is why they used gold, silver, and precious stones as soon as they were in vogue; and given the fact that men had taken away their chances of showing off intellectually, they devoted themselves exclusively to whatever could make them look more attractive. Since that time they have benefited a lot from this; their clothes and their beauty have brought them more esteem than all the books and all the knowledge in the world. The tradition was too well established for any changes to take place subsequently; the practice has continued down to our own day. It seems as if it is a tradition which is too old to find any fault in it.

It seems clear from this historical hypothesis, which is consistent with the normal behaviour of all men, that it was only by power that men retained for themselves those external benefits from which women were excluded. For

What men need to do to justify their treatment of women

in order to be able to say that it was done rationally, it would have to be the case that men share their privileges only with other men who are the most qualified for them, that they select them by means of a just selection procedure, that they admit to studies only those in whom they notice a greater disposition for scientific study, that they appoint to a job only those who are most suitable and that they exclude all others and, finally, that they appoint everyone only to tasks which are most suitable for them.

How men get employment

We see that, in practice, the very opposite happens. It is only chance, necessity or favouritism which gets men appointed to various posts in civil life. Children learn their fathers' trades, because they have heard it spoken about so often. Thus one person is persuaded to become a lawyer although he would much prefer to be a soldier if it were left to his choice; and even the most gifted man in the world would not get an office if he did not have the funds to pay for it.

How many people are there in humble occupations who would have been distinguished if they had got a little encouragement? And how many peasants are there who would be great teachers if they had been put to study? There is no reason to think that those who are most skilled today are those who, in their generation, had the most aptitude for the things in which they excel, and that among such a large number of people enslaved in ignorance, there are none who would have made themselves much more qualified if they had been given the same opportunities as others.

On what basis then could one be certain that women are less gifted than us and that it is not chance, but some insurmountable necessity, which prevents them from participating? I do not claim that they are all suited to the sciences and employments, nor that each one of them is suited to everything. No one would claim that for men either. I only ask that, considering the two sexes in general, one acknowledges as much aptitude in one as in the other.

Consider only what happens in children's games. Girls

show more gentleness, more character, and more skill in them; as long as fear or shame do not smother their thoughts, they speak in a more vivacious and pleasing manner. In their conversations there is more liveliness, more humour and more freedom; they learn whatever they are taught more quickly, as long as they receive comparable instruction; they are more assiduous and more patient at work, more obedient, more modest and more discreet. In a word, one finds in them to a higher degree all those excellent qualities which makes one think, in the case of young men in whom these qualities appear, that they are more suited to great things than their peers.

Comparison of young infants of each sex

Nevertheless, although what is apparent in the two sexes while they are still only in the cradle is already enough to show that the more beautiful of the two also gives the highest hopes, no one takes any account of it. Teachers and instruction are reserved for men. The greatest care is taken to teach them everything which is thought suitable for developing their minds, while women are allowed to languish in idleness, indolence, and ignorance or to remain in the most lowly and vile work.

Besides, one only needs eyes to see that the two sexes are like two brothers in the same family, where the youngest often shows that, despite the neglect with which he was reared, the older son has nothing more than him apart from the advantage of having been born first.

What use is education normally to the men for whom it is provided? For most of them it is useless for the purpose for which it is given. It does not succeed in preventing many from falling into dissoluteness and vice, nor does it prevent others from remaining permanently ignorant or even from becoming more stupid than they were previously. If they have some degree of politeness, cheerfulness or civility, they lose it as a result of studying. Everything clashes with them and they are in conflict with everything. They display so much rudeness and boorishness in their manners at home that one might imagine that, during their youth, they were involved in travelling in a country where they met only savages. What they have learned is like contraband goods, which they could not dare or do

That study is useless for most men

not know how to sell. If they wish to enter into society and play their proper role they have to be taught by ladies[6] in order to learn politeness, kindness and all the outer appearances which are nowadays essential for respectable people.

If one were to examine this more closely, instead of despising women because they do not engage in the sciences, one would consider them lucky. For if, on the one hand, they are thereby deprived of the means of developing their talents and of the benefits which they deserve, on the other hand, they do not have an opportunity for ruining or losing their talents and, despite this privation, they develop in virtue, in mind and in good manners as they grow older. If we compared without prejudice young men when they complete their studies with women of the same age and of comparable intelligence, without knowing how each group had been reared, we would conclude that the women had been given a superior education which was the exact opposite of the men's.

The difference in manners between the two sexes

Even the externals — the appearance of their face, their looks, the way they walk, their demeanour, gestures — all these have a certain sobriety, wisdom and respectability in women which distinguishes them from men. In everything they observe the correct decorum; no one could be more discreet than they are. One never hears a double-meaning word from their lips; the least equivocation hurts their ears, and they cannot bear to see anything which offends modesty.

The majority of men act in exactly the opposite way. Their walking is often hurried, their gestures bizarre, their eyes poorly controlled; and they are never happier than when they discuss and talk about things which should remain secret or hidden.

Comparison of women with the learned

If one engages in conversation with women and with those who are considered learned in society, either with each group separately or with both together, one sees that there is a big difference between the two. One could say that what men put into their heads by study only serves to disturb and confuse their minds. There are very few things which they express clearly, and they have so much trouble in dragging out their words that one loses one's interest in anything worthwhile which they might have to say. And unless they are very keen-minded and in the company of others who are like themselves, they cannot sustain an hour of conversation.

Women, by contrast, express what they know precisely and in an orderly way. Words come easily to them. They begin to speak and continue as they please, and their imagination constantly keeps them supplied without ever running short as long as they are free. They have the gift of expressing their feelings with a sweetness and charm which is as useful as reason for communicating them, whereas men usually express their feelings in a way which is dry and rigid.

If one broaches some subject in the presence of women who are a little educated, they get the point at issue much more quickly. They consider it from more points of view. If one says anything which is true, it takes a firmer hold on their minds. When one gets to know them a bit better and is no longer suspect in their eyes, one finds that their prejudices are not as strong as those of men and they do not use them as much to obstruct whatever truth one proposes. They are far removed from the spirit of contradiction and dispute to which the learned are so subject. They do not cavil vainly about words and they do not use those scientific and mysterious words which are so apt for camouflaging one's ignorance. Everything they say is intelligible and sensible.

I took the opportunity of talking with women of many different conditions whom I was able to meet in the town or in the country, in order to find out their strengths and weaknesses, and I found more common sense in those whom necessity or work had not made stupid than in most works which are much esteemed by the common learned men.

The opinion of a great philosopher

In speaking of God, it never occurred to any woman to tell me that she *imagined God was like a venerable old man*. On the contrary, they said that they could not imagine him — that is, they could not represent him by means of an idea — like a man; that they thought God exists, because they did not think of themselves or of what surrounded them as the work of chance or of some creature; that the conduct of their affairs was not a result of their own prudence and must be the effect of a divine providence, because success was rarely achieved by the strategies which they adopted.

These are the opinions of philosophers

When I asked them what they thought about the soul, they did not reply that it was *a very subtle flame or the disposition of the organs of their body, nor that it was capable of stretching or contracting*. They replied, on the contrary, that they understood well that it was distinct from the body; that the only thing they could say with certainty about it was that they did not believe that it was in any way similar to anything which they perceived by means of the senses and that, if they had studied, they would know precisely what it was.

There is no nurse who would dare say, as the physicians do, that their patients are improving because *the 'digestive faculty' is performing its functions well*;[7] and when they see a large quantity of blood coming from a vein, they laugh at those who deny that there is a connection with the other veins by circulation.[8]

When I wanted to know why they believed that stones exposed to the sun and the rains of the south are more quickly eroded than those in the north, no woman was so simple-minded as to reply that *it happens because the moon chews them up*, as some philosophers imagine rather comically; but they replied that it is the heat of the sun which dries the stones and the sudden rains which soften them more easily.

A scholastic question

I explicitly asked more than twenty women if they believed *that God could cause a stone to be raised to the beatific vision by means of some extraordinary or obediential power*.[9] However, I could get no reply except that they thought I wished to make fun of them with such a question.

Benefits of knowledge

The greatest results which one could hope for from the sciences would be the discernment and precision to distinguish what is true and evident from what is false and obscure, and thereby to avoid falling into error and mistakes. One is inclined to believe that men — at least those who pass as learned men — have an advantage over women in this respect. Nevertheless, if one had a little of this precision which I speak of, one would find that it is one of the qualities which men lack most of all. They are not only obscure and confused in their discourses; it is only because of this obscurity that they often dominate and attract the trust of simple and credulous people. They even reject what is clear and evident, and they despise those who speak in a clear and intelligible manner as too simple and common. They are the first to fall into whatever obscurity is proposed to them as if it were something which is more mysterious. In order to become convinced of this, all one needs to do is to listen to them with a little attention and ask them to explain themselves.

Women have mental precision

Women have a disposition which is far removed from that. One notices that women who have a little experience of the world cannot bear to have even their children speak Latin in their presence. They distrust others who speak Latin, and say rather frequently that they fear that there is some impertinence hidden under these foreign clothes. Not only does one not hear them pronounce those terms which have been sanctioned by the sciences; they cannot even remember them, despite the fact that they have a good memory and the words have been repeated to them often. When one speaks obscurely to them, they claim in good faith that they do not have enough intelligence or mental ability to understand what is said to them, or else they realise that those who speak to them in this way are not adequately educated.

Finally, if one considered the manner in which men and women express what they know, one would see that men are like workers who labour with difficulty on stones which are completely rough and shapeless; and that women are like those architects or skilled stonemasons who know how to polish and set with ease, in their proper places, whatever stones they have available.

Not only are there a great number of women who can

judge things as if they had been given a better education, without the prejudices or confusions which are so common among the learned, but there are many who have such sound judgement that they speak about the subject-matter of the most advanced sciences as if they had studied them all their lives.

Women have the art of talking

Women express themselves gracefully. They have the art of finding the most appropriate terms in use and of communicating more in one word than men can with many words. And if one discusses languages in general with women, they have ideas about that subject which are found only among the most gifted grammarians. Finally, one can see that they learn more about language simply by using it than most men can derive from the use of language together with study.

Women are eloquent

Eloquence is a talent which is so natural to women and so characteristic of them that no one could dispute it. They convince one of anything they wish. They know how to accuse and defend without having studied law, and there are hardly any judges who have not experienced that they are as good as lawyers. Could there be anything which is stronger and more eloquent than the writing of some women about everything which is involved in daily life, and especially the passions, the force of which shows all the beauty and skill of eloquence? They describe the passions in a way which is so subtle and they express them so simply that one has to agree that one does not experience the passions in any other way, and that all the rhetorical treatises in the world could not teach men what women are capable of doing without the least difficulty. Works of eloquence or poetry, orations, sermons and discourses, are not too sophisticated for their taste and there is nothing lacking in their critiques except to express them according to the terms and rules of the art.

I certainly hope that this treatise will not escape their criticism either, that many will find something to criticise in it. Some may find that it is not adequate to the importance and dignity of the subject-matter; looking through it they will find it is not complimentary enough, that the style is not noble enough, nor the expression strong and lofty enough. Others may find that there are things which are inadequately dealt with, to which one could add other important comments. However I also hope that my good will, and my plan not to say anything which is not true and to avoid expressions which are too strong so as not to sound like a novel, will excuse me in their eyes.

They have the eloquence of action

Women also have this advantage that the eloquence of action is more developed in them than in men. In order to find out what they want, it is enough to see from their bearing what they plan to touch. They have a noble and lofty appearance, a free and majestic bearing, a proper deportment, natural gestures and engaging manners, a facility with speech and a gentle and flexible voice. The beauty and grace which go hand in hand with their speaking, whenever they become animated, open up one's heart to them. When they speak of good and evil, one sees on their face the sign of virtue which increases their persuasiveness. And whenever they decide to direct their love towards virtue, their love is manifest in their speech; the idea of virtue which they express, clothed in the adornments of the speech and elegance which is characteristic of them, appears a hundred times more beautiful.

They know the law and understand how to practise it

It is a pleasure to hear a woman who gets involved in legal pleading. They dissipate and explain succinctly whatever confusion is present in a case. A woman explains exactly her claims and those of the party she represents. She makes clear what gave rise to the legal case, the way in which she conducts it, the various avenues by which she has tried to resolve it, and all the procedures which she followed. One finds in all of this a clear ability for legal causes which the majority of men lack.

That is what makes me think that, if they studied law, they would succeed at least as well as us men. One sees that they have a greater love for peace and justice; they tolerate disputes with difficulty and they gladly intervene in order to conclude them amicably. Their care helps them find a special slant or expedient in order to reconcile minds; and in running their own households or those of others, they naturally apply the basic rules of equity on which the whole of jurisprudence is based.

In the accounts which are given even by women of modest ability, there is always an indefinable pleasantness

They have an aptitude for history

which has a greater impact than in the accounts given by us men. They know how to distinguish what is appropriate or inappropriate to a subject, to disentangle the interests involved, to identify the character of the personalities, to uncover their intrigues and follow both the major and the minor ones once they have identified them. All of this can be seen even more in the histories and novels of learned women who are alive today.

They know theology

How many women learn as much from sermons, conversations and small books of piety as the doctors of theology learn from St Thomas in their study or in the schools? The conviction and depth with which they speak about the deepest mysteries and about the whole of Christian morality is such that they would often be taken for great theologians, if only they had a theologian's hat and if they could cite a few passages in Latin.

They understand medicine

It seems as if women are born to practise medicine and to restore health to the sick. Their cleanliness and kindness go half-way towards relieving ailments. They are skilled not only in applying remedies, but also in discovering them. They discover thousands of remedies which are described as insignificant because they cost much less than those of Hippocrates and are not officially prescribed.[10] However, the former are much more reliable and simple because they are natural. Finally, women make observations in their practice with so much care, and by reasoning so well, that they often make all schoolbooks useless.

Women know the opposite to astrological fantasies

The vagaries of the seasons are well known to country women who work in the fields. Their almanacs are much more reliable than those which are printed from the pen of astrologers. They explain the fertility and infertility of the years so artlessly by reference to the winds, rains, and everything which affects the weather, that one could not listen to them on this subject without being sorry for the learned who explain these phenomena by reference to the aspects, the conjunctions and the ascendants of the planets. This makes me think that if they had been taught that the changes to which the human body is subject can occur as a result of its own make-up, or from exercise, climate, nourishment, education and various life experi-

The origin of the diversity of habits and inclinations

ences, they would never dare to explain its inclinations or changes by reference to the influence of the stars, which are bodies which are many millions of leagues away from us.[11]

Why women do not speak about some sciences

It is true that there are sciences that women do not talk about, because they are not practical sciences or sciences about society. Algebra, geometry, optics rarely emerge from the studies or learned academies and appear in the midst of everyday life; and since they are primarily useful in making our thinking precise, they should hardly appear in ordinary life except discreetly, like the hidden springs which make large machines work. That is to say that one should apply these sciences to everyday topics, and that we should think and speak accurately and geometrically without seeming to be geometricians.

All this is more evident in ladies

All these observations on qualities of the mind can be applied without difficulty to women of relatively modest social status, but if one goes as high as the Court and engages in conversation with ladies, one can notice something very different. It seems as if their intelligence is naturally commensurate with their social status. With their accuracy, discernment, and politeness, they have an intellectual grasp which is keen, delicate and relaxed and there is something lofty and noble which is characteristic of them. One might say that things, just like men, approach them only with respect. They always see things in their best light, and in speaking about them they give a much different impression than what is commonly given. In a word, if one shows two letters from women of different social status to someone who is sufficiently sensitive, he will easily recognise which of them is from a lady of higher social standing.

Learned women, who are very numerous, are more worthy of esteem than learned men

How many women have there been and how many are there still who should be numbered among the learned, unless of course one wished to rank them even higher? The century in which we live has more learned women than all past centuries taken together, and since they have equalled men they are more worthy of esteem than men for very special reasons. They had to overcome the indolence in which they were reared, renounce the pleasures and laziness to which they had been reduced, overcome a number of public obstacles which kept them from study, and also overcome the unfavourable ideas which common folk have about learned women, apart from those which they have about the female sex in general. They have done all that; and whether it is true that the obstacles made their minds more lively and penetrating, or whether these qualities are natural to them, they have become proportionately more clever than men.

It must be recognised that, in general, women are capable of scientific work

One could say, nevertheless, without lessening the praise which these illustrious women deserve, that it is chance and external conditions which have put them in this favourable situation, just like the most learned among us men, and that there are innumerable other women who would have done just as well if they had been given equal opportunities. And just as it is rather unfair to believe that all women are indiscreet simply because one knows five or six women who are so, in a similar way one should be equally fair and judge that their sex is capable of scientific study because there have been a number of women who have succeeded in getting that far.

It is commonly believed that the Turks, the barbarians and savages are not as capable of study as the peoples of Europe. However, it is certain that if one saw five or six of them who had the ability or the title of doctor — which is not impossible — one would correct one's judgement and admit that these people are men just like us, are capable of the same things and that, if they were instructed, they would be equal to us in everything. The women with whom we live are as important as the barbarians and savages, important enough to compel us to have opinions about them which are neither less favourable nor less reasonable.

If common folk believe, despite these observations, that women are not as suited to the sciences as we are, they should at least recognise that the sciences are not as necessary for women. They apply themselves to the sciences for two reasons: one is to understand those matters which the sciences study, and the other is to become virtuous by means of the knowledge thereby acquired. Thus, in this life which is so short, science should be directed exclusively towards virtue; and since women already possess virtue one could say that, by a unique good fortune, they have the principal benefit of the sciences without having studied them.

Women are just as virtuous as men

What we see every day should convince us that women are just as Christian as men. They accept the Gospel with humility and simplicity. They practise the Gospel maxims to an exemplary degree. Their respect for everything to do with religion has always seemed to be so great that they are accepted, without challenge, as being more devout and pious than us. It is true that their devotion sometimes becomes excessive; however, I do not find this excess blameworthy. The ignorance in which they are reared is an adequate explanation of it.[12] If their zeal is indiscreet, at least their faith is genuine; and one could say that, since they cling to virtue so strongly even in the darkness of ignorance, if they understood virtue perfectly they would embrace it very differently.

They are charitable

It seems as if the Gospel virtue of compassion were destined for their sex. News of their neighbour's misfortune hardly reaches their ears when it touches their hearts and brings tears to their eyes. Is it not their hands which have always distributed the most during public calamities? Is it not the ladies who in our own day have special care of the poor and the sick in the parishes, who visit them in prisons and who look after them in hospitals? Is it not the pious sisters scattered in the various parts of the town who have the responsibility of bringing them nourishment and necessary medicines at certain times of the day, and to whom the name of charity — which they exercise so worthily — has been given?[13]

The Daughters of Charity

The Sisters of the Hôtel-Dieu

Finally, when the time comes when there are no women in the world who practise the virtue of charity towards their neighbours apart from those who look after the sick in the Hôtel-Dieu, I do not believe that men could justly pretend that they have an advantage in this over women.[14] It is exactly those women who would enhance the gallery of heroic women,[15] it is their lives that would have to be celebrated with the greatest praise, and it is their deaths which one would have to honour with the most excellent panegyrics. For it is here that one can see the Christian religion, i.e. truly heroic virtue, being practised rigorously according to the commandments and the counsels. One can see young women renounce the world and themselves, committed to permanent chastity and poverty, taking up their cross, and the most difficult cross of the world, in order to place themselves for the rest of their lives under the yoke of Jesus Christ. They consecrate themselves in a hospital where all sorts of sick people, of every country or religion, are welcomed with respect, in order to serve them without discrimination and to follow the example of their spouse [i.e. Christ] by taking care of all sorts of human sickness, without being disgusted by seeing constantly the most atrocious sights, by hearing the cries of the injured and by smelling all the infections of the human body. It is characteristic of the spirit which inspires them that they carry the sick from one bed to another in their arms and that they encourage the unfortunates, not with empty words, but with an effective and personal example of patience and of indomitable charity.

Could anyone imagine anything greater among Christians? Other women are no less inclined to comfort their neighbours. The only thing they lack is the opportunity, and other tasks distract them. I think it is just as unwarranted to conclude from this — as is commonly done — that women are naturally subservient to men, as it is to pretend that those who get special gifts from God are the servants or slaves of all those for whose benefit they use these gifts.

How women live in celibacy

Whatever lifestyle women adopt, their conduct always includes some remarkable features. It appears that those who live unmarried lives while still living in society remain there only in order to provide an example for others. Christian modesty is manifest in their faces and in their behaviour. Virtue is their principal adornment. They avoid worldly companionships and distractions. Their dedication to works of piety shows clearly that they are not involved in the cares and demands of marriage, so that they can enjoy a much greater freedom of mind and not be bound to anything except pleasing God.

How they live in convents

There are as many monasteries under the control of women as there are under the control of men, and the lives of women in convents are no less exemplary. Their retreat from the world is greater; their penitence is more austere, and abbesses are as good as abbots. They make rules with admirable wisdom and govern their spiritual daughters with such prudence that no disorder ever arises. Finally, the fame of religious houses, the great wealth which they possess, and their solid buildings are the result of the good order with which their superiors manage them.

How women live in the married state

Marriage is the most natural state and the most usual one for mankind. Once people embark on it, it is for the rest of their lives. They live in marriage through those stages of their lives in which one ought to act only by reason. The various accidents of nature or fortune to which marriage is subject, which apply to a greater extent to those in this state, give them an opportunity of showing more intelligence. It does not require a wide experience to realise that women are more suited to marriage than we are. Young women are able to manage a home at an age when men still need a tutor, and the most common expedient for training a young man in good behaviour is to give him a woman who will restrain him by her example, moderate his fits of passion and withdraw him from debauchery.

What accomodating kindness women must exercise in order to live in peace with their husbands! They submit to their commands, do nothing without their advice, restrain themselves in many things so as not to displease them, and they often deprive themselves of the most innocent enjoyments in order to avoid suspicion. It is well known which of the two sexes is more faithful to the other and supports more patiently the difficulties which occur in marriage, and which of them demonstrates more wisdom in these difficulties.

Most homes are managed by women, to whom the men have relinguished their management. The care which they

How women rear their children

exercise in educating their children is much more significant for the families and more important for the state than the care they take of property. They apply themselves totally to the protection of their children. They have such great fear that some evil might befall their children that they often lose sleep over it. They deprive themselves willingly of necessary things so that their children will not want for anything. They cannot see them suffer in the slightest without suffering themselves in the very depths of their soul. One could say that their greatest suffering is not being able to console their children when they are taking care of their pains.

Their solicitude for their children's education

Who is unaware of the dedication with which women work to instruct their children in virtue, in so far as their young age will allow? They try to make them know and love God, and they teach them to adore God in a way which is appropriate for them. They take care to put them under the guidance of a tutor as soon as they are ready for it, and they choose their tutor with the greatest care in order to improve their education. And, what is ever more praiseworthy, they combine good example with their instruction.

That a more extensive consideration of details would be to the advantage of women

If one wished to go into great detail and to examine the more important features of all life's stages and all the virtues which women practise in them, then one would find material for a very extensive eulogy. One could show how far their sobriety goes in the use of food and drink, their patience in coping with difficulties, and their strength and courage in bearing with suffering, tiredness, sleeplessness and fasting; their moderation in pleasure and the emotions; their inclination to do good; their prudence in business affaris and their virtue in everything. In a word, one could show that there is no virtue which they do not have in common with us and that, on the contrary, there is a considerable number of faults which are peculiar to us men.

These are my general and common observations about women as regard their qualities of mind, the use of which is the only thing which gives rise to a distinction between human beings.

Since there are hardly any situations in life in which one could not discover the inclination, disposition, vice or virtue, and the ability of people, those who wish to correct their views about women always have an opportunity of doing so, either in public or in private, at the court or at the convent grille, in entertainments or in religious life, among the rich or the poor, in whatever state or condition women might be. If one examined impartially and honestly what can be observed about women one would find that, although there may be a few things which seem to be less favourable to them, there are many more which are very much to their advantage. One would also see that it is not because of a lack of merit on their part, but because of misfortune and a lack of strength, that their condition is not equal to ours; and finally, that the common belief about women is a widespread and ill-founded prejudice.

Part II

Which shows why the evidence that can be used against the equality of the sexes, which is taken from poets, orators, historians, jurists and philosophers, is completely frivolous and useless

Common folk are convinced of their views about women because they realise that their views are supported by the opinions of the learned. Thus as long as the public utterances of those who have authority based on trust are in agreement with certain general appearances, to the detriment of women, one should not be surprised to find such mistaken beliefs among people who are simple and unlearned. Thus it happens, as in so many different things, that one gets deeper into one prejudice by means of another.[16]

Since the concept of truth is related naturally to that of scientific knowledge, whatever is proposed by those who have a reputation for being learned is always accepted as the truth. And since the number of those who are wise in name only is much greater than the number of those who are genuinely wise, the majority of people — who decide issues simply by the number of people who support them — believe the former; they also accept their views more readily to the extent that they happen to agree with what they themselves already believe.

The opinion of popular knowledge

That is why when common folk see poets, orators, historians and philosophers also claiming that women are inferior to men, that they are less noble and less perfect, they become more convinced of this belief; for they do not realise that the science [of historians, etc.] is the same prejudice as their own, except that it is more long-winded and specious, and that learned people do nothing more than add to the commonly accepted opinion the beliefs of the ancients, on whose authority all their certitude depends. I find that, on the question of the sexes, both those who studied and those who have not studied fall into exactly the same mistake; i.e. they believe that what is said about this issue by those whom they respect is true, because they have decided in advance that they speak the truth; however, they should not be willing to believe what they say before they have made sure that they say only what is true.

Against the authority of poets and orators

Since the objective of poets and orators is merely to please and persuade, all they need to know — as far as most people are concerned — is how things seem to be. Since exaggeration and hyperbole are most appropriate for this objective, allowing one to magnify ideas according to one's needs, they make good and evil big or small as they wish. By a much too common twist, they attribute to all women in general what they observe in only a few in particular. It is enough for them to have seen a few hypocrites among women to say that the entire female sex is subject to the same fault. The embellishments with which they accompany their discourse contribute very much to attract the credulity of those who are not careful. They speak with facility and elegance and they exploit various stylistic devices which, being attractive, pleasant and unusual, dazzle the mind and hinder it from discerning the truth. There are a number of pieces written about women which, on first impression, are very convincing; people believe them because they do not realise that what makes them persuasive and apparently true are the figures of speech, the metaphors and proverbs, the descriptions, similitudes and emblems which they contain. Because there is usually much skill and wit in writings like this, one assumes that they also contain as much truth.

One person might believe that women like to be deceived because he read Sarasin's sonnet about the fall of the first woman, which pretends that she would not have fallen had she not listened to the sweet nothings of the Devil.[17] It is true that this image is humorous, the story is a good one, the use to which it is put is appropriate in the context and the Fall is very pleasant. However if the poem is examined in depth and translated into prose, it becomes clear that there is nothing which is more false or insipid.

There are some people who are simple-minded enough to imagine that women are more inclined to anger than men, because they read how the poets represented the Furies in the form of women; but they fail to notice that this is a simple poetic construction and that paintings which depict shrews with a woman's face also depict the Devil under the guise of a man.

I have seen attempts to show that women are fickle on the basis of what a famous Latin poet said, i.e. that they are subject to continual changes, and on the basis of a Frenchman's humorous comparison of women with a weather-vane which moves with the wind; these arguments failed to notice that all these ways of talking are useful only for misleading the mind rather than for instructing it.

Common eloquence is a verbal optics which makes things appear as if they had any shape or colour one wishes, and there is no virtue which could not be represented as a vice by using the means which it provides.

There is nothing more common among authors than the idea that women are less perfect and less noble than men. However, they have no reason at all for believing this. It very much seems as if they were persuaded of this opinion in the same way as common folk were. Women do not share with us in those external advantages, such as the sciences or positions of authority, by which people usually measure perfection. They conclude, therefore, that they are not as perfect as we are. However, to be convinced of this for certain, one would have to show that they are excluded from such benefits because they are not suited to them. But it is not as easy to show this as one might imagine, and it will not be difficult to demonstrate the contrary in what follows and to show that this mistake stems from the fact that one has only a confused idea of perfection and nobility.

All the arguments of those who hold that the fair sex is not as noble or as excellent as ours are based on the assumption that, since men are in authority, it must be the case that everything is for their benefit. I am certain that the very opposite would be believed with even greater conviction, i.e. that men are only there for the sake of women, if women had all the authority, as is the case in the Amazons' empire.[18]

It is true that women only have jobs here which are regarded as the lowest. It is also true that, as far as reason or religion are concerned, they should not be less esteemed than men. There is nothing lower than vice, nor more noble than virtue. Since women show more virtue than men, even in their humble occupations, they deserve to be more highly regarded than men. I am not even sure that, considering only their usual work which is to nourish and rear children in their infancy, they are not worthy of the highest rank in civil society.

That women are more valuable than men in respect of their work

If we were free as individuals and without a commonwealth, we would not come together in a group except in order better to protect our lives and to enjoy peacefully those things which are necessary for this purpose.[19] We would value more those people who contributed more to our objective. That is why we have got used to considering princes as the first in the state, because their care and foresight is the most extensive and the most general, and we rank those who are below them accordingly. Most people give priority to soldiers rather than judges, because soldiers directly confront those who threaten life in the most terrifying ways, and everyone values people in so far as they consider them useful. Therefore, women would seem to be the most valuable, because the service which they provide is incomparably greater than that of anyone else.

How much should women be valued?

One could do without princes, soldiers, and merchants completely, as people did at the beginning of the world and as savages still do today. But one could not do without women in one's infancy. Once states are completely at peace, the majority of the people who exercise authority seem to be almost dead or useless. Women, however, never cease to be necessary. Justice officials are useful only to protect the property of owners; women are there to protect life for us. Soldiers are at the service of mature human beings who are capable of defending themselves, whereas women are at the service of people at a time when they still do not know who they are or whether they have enemies or friends, and when they have no defence apart from their tears against those who might attack them. Teachers, magistrates, or princes often act only for their own glory and their personal benefit, whereas women act only in the interests of the children whom they rear. Finally, the pains and care, the fatigue and consideration which women assume are unmatched in any other office in civil society.

Therefore, it is pure fantasy which makes them less valued than men. A man who tamed a tiger would be rewarded generously. Those who know how to train horses, monkeys or elephants are highly valued; a man who writes a little book, which hardly takes any time or effort, is spoken highly of. Women, however, are neglected although they spend many years in nourishing and educating children. If one looked carefully for the reason why, one would find that it is because one job is more common than the other.

Against the evidence which might be gleaned from history

What historians say unfavourably about women has a greater impact on our minds than the discourses of orators; their evidence is less suspect because they appear not to propose any of their own opinions. Besides, it corresponds to what people already believe, namely that in earlier times women were the same as people think they are today. However all the authority which historians have over people's minds is merely the effect of a prejudice about antiquity which is fairly common; antiquity is pictured as an old man who, since he is very wise and experienced, is incapable of being mistaken or saying anything which is false.

However, the ancients were no less human than we are nor less subject to error, and one should not accept their opinions today any more than one should have done in their own time. Women were thought of in former times as they are today, and with just as little justification. Thus everything which men say about women should be suspect because they are both judges and litigants.[20] When someone quotes the opinions of a thousand authors against women, this history should be considered as nothing more than a tradition of prejudices and errors. There is as little accuracy and truth is ancient histories as there is in popular stories, in which it is well known that there is almost none. Those who wrote the histories inserted their own emotions and concerns into them, and many of those authors had only a very confused idea of vice and virtue and often took one for the other. Those who read them without taking special care fall into the same mistake. Given their prejudices, the ancients were careful to exaggerate the virtues and merits of their own sex and, in contrast, to downplay and weaken the merits of women. This is so easy to recognise that it is unnecessary to give examples.

Historical evidence in favour of women

However if one is able to disentangle the past a little, one finds enough to show that women were not surpassed by men and that the virtue which women displayed is greater if one considers it accurately in all its circumstances. One can see that women showed equally convincing signs of intelligence and ability in all kinds of contexts. There were some women who ruled large states and empires with a degree of wisdom and moderation which was unparalleled; others dispensed justice with an integrity equal to that of the Areopagus.[21] Many, by their prudence and their advice, re-established peace in their kingdoms or put their husbands back on their thrones. They have been seen leading armies, or defending themselves on the ramparts with more than heroic courage. How many women have there been whose chastity could not be compromised either by appalling threats or by the wonderful promises which were made to them, and who suffered the most horrible torments with surprising magnanimity for the sake of their religion? How many women have there been who became as competent as men in all the sciences, who have delved into what is most obscure in nature, what is most subtle in politics and what is most fundamental in morality, or who reached the highest levels in Christian theology? Thus the history which is used by those who are biased against women in order to debase their sex can help those who examine it impartially to show that the female sex is no less noble than ours.

Against lawyers

The authority of lawyers carries a lot of weight with many people in regard to women because lawyers make a special profession of giving everyone their due. They put women under the power of their husbands like children under the control of their fathers, and then say that it is nature which assigned the lowest functions in society to women and kept them out of public office.

People think that, in repeating what lawyers say, they are on firm ground. But it is possible to disagree with lawyers on this point without diminishing the respect which they deserve. One would embarrass them seriously if they were forced to explain intelligibly what they mean by 'nature' in this context, and to explain how nature distinguishes the two sexes in the ways they imagine.

One must assume that those who made the laws, being men, discriminated in favour of their own sex, as women might have done had they been in their place. As far as women are concerned, laws were made from the time when societies were founded in the same way as they are today; thus lawyers — who also had their own prejudices — have attributed to nature a distinction which derives only from custom. Besides, it was not necessary to change the regime which they found already established in order to attain their own objective, which was to govern the state well by dispensing justice. Finally, if they are so obstinate in believing that women are naturally inferior to men, one could argue with them on the basis of their own principles, because they themselves should be able to see that dependency and servitude are against the natural order which makes all human beings equal.

Since subordination is a purely physical or civil relation, it should be considered only as an effect of chance, violence or custom, apart from the dependent relationship of children on those who gave them life. Besides, is there not a certain age at which human beings, being presumed to have enough reason and experience to govern themselves, are released by law from the authority of others?

However, between people of more or less the same age

there should be only a reasonable subordination by which those who are less knowledgeable submit themselves voluntarily to those who are more so. Thus if one were to remove the legal privileges which laws confer on men and which make them the heads of their families, the only kind of subordination remaining between men and women would be one based on experience and knowledge. Both men and women commit themselves to each other freely at a time when women are as reasonable as, and sometimes more reasonable than, their husbands. The promises and conventions of marriage are reciprocal and their marital rights are equal. Thus if the law gives husbands more authority over their property, nature gives women more power and rights over the children. Since the will of one partner is not binding on the other, if the woman is obliged to do those things which her husband requests, the latter is no less obliged to do what the wife indicates as his duty. Apart from reasonable requests, one cannot constrain a woman to be subject to her husband just because she is not as strong as he is. This is what is called acting like a Turk to a Moor,[22] and not like an intelligent human being.

Against philosophers

There is little difficulty in refuting the views of those learned people about whom I have just been speaking, for one can easily see that their work does not require them to become well informed about the real nature of things and that, in order to realise their objectives, poets and orators are satisfied with appearances and how things seem to be, just as the evidence of antiquity suffices for historians or custom suffices for lawyers. As far as the opinions of philosophers are concerned, however, one cannot dismiss them so easily, for it seems as if they are above all the preceding considerations, as indeed they ought to be, and they are thought to examine matters much more closely. This attracts the credulity of common folk and makes philosophers' opinions seem indubitable, especially when they agree with the opinions which one already holds.

Thus common folk become more convinced of their belief that the sexes are unequal, because they see those whose opinions they consider a guide for themselves holding the same view; they do not realise that most philosophers have no guide over and above what is available to common folk, and that it is not as a result of some science that they make their pronouncements, especially on this particular question. They brought their prejudices into the schools and learned nothing there which would help to cure them of their prejudices. On the contrary, all their knowledge is based on judgements which they made since childhood and they consider it a crime or a mistake to cast doubt on anything which they believed before the age of reason. They are not taught to understand human nature by means of the body or the soul; instead, what they usually teach about human nature could very well serve to show that there is only a difference of degree between us and animals. They are never told anything about the sexes, because it is assumed that they already know enough about them; they are far from examining the abilities of the sexes and the natural and genuine differences between them, which is a very interesting issue and may well be more important than physics or morals. They spend entire years and some of them their whole lives with trifles and beings of reason,[23] or wondering if there are imaginary spaces above the earth, or whether atoms or the small particles of dust which can be seen in the sunlight are infinitely divisible. How can we rely on what learned men of this kind say when it comes to science and important issues?

School philosophers

One might think, however, that even though they are so poorly taught, the principles of scholastic philosophers might be used to discover which of the two sexes is naturally superior to the other. But this idea would only occur either to those who do not know their principles, or to those who are already committed to them. Knowledge of ourselves is absolutely necessary in order to discuss this issue, especially knowledge of the body which is the organ of the sciences, just as, in order to understand how telescopes make things larger, one must understand how they are made. Scholastic philosophers never speak about the body except in passing, no more than they speak about truth and about science, i.e. the method for acquiring true and certain knowledge, without which it is impossible to consider properly if women are just as capable as we are of acquiring such knowledge. Without taking the time to report the suggestions which they make about this issue, I will say what I think about them in a general way.

What is science

All human beings are made alike, they have the same sensations and the same ideas of natural objects, for example, of light, heat, or hardness. All the science which we try to acquire about these things is nothing more than knowing truly, with respect to each object, what are the internal and external dispositions which produce in us the sensations and ideas which we have of it. The most that teachers can do for us in order to lead us to this knowledge is to apply our minds to what we notice so as to examine its appearances and its effects, without hurry or prejudice, and to show us the order which we should follow in arranging our thoughts so as to find what we are looking for.

What is liquidity

For example, if an unlearned person asked me to explain to him the liquidity of water, I would not tell him anything. Instead I would ask him what he had observed; for instance, that if water is not enclosed in a vase, it spreads out, that is to say, that all its parts separate and dissociate one from another, without any other body being introduced; that one can put one's fingers into it without difficulty and without experiencing the resistance of hard bodies; and that when sugar or salt is put into water, one finds that these kinds of body gradually get smaller and that small parts of them are transported to all parts of the liquid.

Up to this point I have taught him nothing. If I got him to understand rest and motion in a similar way, I would get him to realise that the nature of liquids consists in the fact that their invisible parts are in perpetual motion, that this requires them to be enclosed in a container and makes liquids such that they easily allow for the insertion of hard objects. Since the parts of water are small, smooth, and narrow, they insinuate themselves into the pores of sugar, thereby disturbing and dividing its parts by their action and, since they move in every direction, they carry off into every corner of the container those parts of the sugar which they have broken off.

This idea of liquids, which is a section detached from the body of physics, would be much clearer if it were seen in context. It contains nothing which ordinary women could not understand. If all the rest of our knowledge were introduced in an orderly way, it would cause no greater difficulty; and if one paid attention, one would see that every rational science requires less intelligence and less time than is necessary for learning embroidery or needlework well.

One requires as much intelligence to learn embroidery or needlework as to learn physics

In fact, the ideas of natural things are necessary and they always occur in us in the same way.[24] Adam had them just as we do; children have these ideas in the same way as old men, and women have them just like men. These ideas are repeated, are strengthened and linked together by the constant use of the senses. The mind is always at work; whoever understands well how it operates on one thing also discovers without difficulty how it operates on all the others. There is only a difference of degree between the sensation of the sun and that of a spark; to think clearly about the sun requires neither skill nor physical training.

It is not the same with the crafts which I spoke about. One needs to apply one's mind much more to them. Since the ideas we have of them are variable, it is more difficult both to acquire them and to remember them. If some trade presupposes a lot of practice, then it takes a lot longer to learn it. It requires skill to maintain proportion on a canvas, to distribute the wool and silk evenly, to combine colours appropriately, not to crowd the points together nor separate them too much, so as not to have more in one row than another and to make imperceptible changes in shade. In short, one has to know how to make craftworks and how to vary them in a thousand different ways in order to become skilled at them; in the sciences, however, all one has to do is to observe in an orderly way pieces of workmanship in nature which have already been completely made and are always uniform. The whole difficulty in succeeding at the sciences comes, not so much from the objects studied nor the disposition of the body, but from the limited ability of teachers.

Therefore one should not be surprised any more at unlearned men and women discussing things which pertain to the sciences, because the method for learning sciences is nothing more than an improvement of common sense, which can be confused by haste, custom or usage.

The concept of science which I have proposed in general terms should be enough to persuade thoughtful people that men and women are equally competent to study the sciences. However, since the opposite view is so entrenched it is necessary, in order to become completely freed of it, to tackle it with principles. Thus by combining the physical explanations which are about to be introduced with the qualities which are characteristic of the fair sex, which we saw in the first part, one can be totally convinced of the thesis.

When viewed from the point of view of the principles of a sound philosophy, women are as capable as men of every kind of knowledge

The mind has no sex

It is easy to see that sexual differences apply only to the body since, properly speaking, it is only the body which is used for human reproduction; the mind is involved in reproduction only in giving its assent and, since it does this in the same way in everyone, one may conclude that it has no sex.[25]

It is equal in all human beings

If one considers the mind in itself, one finds that it is equal and has the same nature in all human beings, and that it is capable of all kinds of thoughts. The smallest thoughts occupy the mind in the same way as greater ones; one does not need a smaller thought to understand a mite than to know an elephant. Whoever knows what light and the fire of a spark are also knows what the light of the sun is. When one is used to thinking only about things which pertain to the mind, one understands them all at least as clearly as those things which are more material and which are known through the senses. I do

Source of the differences between people

not see any greater difference between the mind of an uncouth and unlearned man and that of a more refined and enlightened man, than between the mind of the same man at the age of ten and at the age of forty. Since there seems to be just as little difference in the minds of men and women, one can say that the difference between the sexes does not result from their minds. The make-up of the body, but especially education, training, and the perception of everything in our environment are above all the natural and reasonable causes of so many of the differences which can be seen between the sexes.

The mind works in women in the same way as in men

It is God who joins the mind to the body of a woman, as he does to that of a man, and he joins it according to the same laws. It is our sensations, our passions, and our acts of will which constitute and maintain this union; since the mind does not work differently in one sex than in the other, it is equally capable of the same things in each one.

Things are perceived in the same manner by both sexes

This is even more obvious if we consider the head, which is the unique organ of the sciences and the place where the mind exercises all its functions. Our most accurate anatomical investigations do not uncover any difference between men and women in this part of the body. The brain of women is exactly like ours. Sensory impressions are received in the brain and are combined in the same way; they are stored for the imagination and memory in the same way. Women hear by means of their ears, as we do; they see with their eyes and taste with their tongue; there is nothing unusual in the disposition of these organs in women except that they are usually more refined than in men, which is an advantage. Thus external objects affect them in the same way as they affect us, light through the eyes and sound through the ears. What would prevent them, therefore, from applying themselves to

Women are capable of metaphysics

study their own selves, from examining what the nature of the mind is, how many different kinds of thoughts there are, and how ideas are triggered on the occasion of certain bodily movements; what would prevent them from referring to the natural ideas which they have of God and, beginning with spiritual things, from arranging their ideas in order and engaging in the science called metaphysics?

They are capable of physics and medicine

Since they also have eyes and hands, could they not do a dissection of the human body themselves or see one being done by someone else, and consider the body's symmetry and structure, notice the diversity, differences and relations of its parts, their shapes, motions and functions, the changes to which they are subject, and conclude from all this what is necessary to maintain bodies in good condition and to restore them if they ever change.

In order to do that, all they need would be to know the nature of those external bodies which have any connection with our own bodies, to discover their properties and everything about them which makes them capable of having either a good or a bad effect on us. That is known by using our senses and by means of the various experiments which are done on external bodies. Since women are equally capable of both sciences, they can learn physics and medicine as well as we can.

Does one need so much intelligence to know that respiration is absolutely necessary for the conservation of life, that it works by means of the air which enters through the nasal passage and the mouth, goes into the lungs in order to refresh the blood which passes through there in circulating, and which causes various changes in the lungs depending on whether the air is more or less thick as a result of the mixture of vapours and exhalations with which it is sometimes seen to be mixed?

What is taste?

Is it something so difficult to discover that, in so far as the body is concerned, the taste of foods consists in the different ways in which they are dissolved by saliva on the tongue? There is no one who fails to notice that any meat that is eaten after a meal causes a much less pleasant sensation in the mouth, because it breaks up into little parts in a way which is very different from the meat that had been eaten during the meal. Whatever remains to be known about the functions of the human body, when it is considered in a methodical way, does not present any greater difficulty than this.

Women can understand the passions[26]

The passions are surely what is most interesting in this context. One can notice two things here, the motions of the body and the thoughts and feelings of the soul which are linked with them. Women can know this just as well as men. As regards the causes which arouse the passions, one knows how they operate as soon as one understands — as a result of studying physics — the way in which things in our environment enter into our bodies and affect us and, by experience and usage, how we add to or separate from these bodily affections our acts of will.

Women can learn logic

In making regular reflections on the objects studied by the three sciences which we have just spoken of, a woman can notice that the order of her thoughts should follow the order of nature, that her thoughts are accurate as long as they conform to nature, and that precipitation is the only obstacle to accuracy in our judgements. Afterwards, by noticing the method which she followed in order to reach this point, she could do some reflection which would provide her with a guide for the future, and thereby she could construct a logic.

If one insisted, nevertheless, that women could not acquire these kinds of knowledge themselves — which is a purely gratuitous assumption — at least one could not deny that they could acquire them with the help of teachers and books, as the most accomplished men have done in every age.

Mathematics

It is enough to advert to the well-known neatness of the female sex to show that women are capable of understanding mathematical relations. We would contradict ourselves by doubting that they would succeed as well as we do if they applied themselves to making machines, because we attribute to them more skill and dexterity than to ourselves.

They are capable of astronomy

All one needs are eyes and a little attention in order to observe natural phenomena, to notice that the sun and all the luminous bodies in the sky are real fires because they affect us and illuminate us in the same way as fires here on earth; that they seem to correspond successively to different places on earth and, in this way, one can identify their movements and their paths. Whoever can imagine a large-scale model in his head and can get all its wheels turning, can also get the whole machine of the world running accurately in his head if he ever observed carefully its diverse appearances.

Differences between the sciences

We have already found that women have all the dispositions which make men suitable for the sciences, when the sciences are considered in themselves. If we proceed to look at the matter more closely, we will also find that women have those dispositions which are necessary for the sciences when they are considered as linked with similar undertakings in civil society.

It is a mistake of the common philosophy so to emphasise differences between the sciences that one can hardly see any connection between them in terms of the method which is characteristic of the sciences.[27] This is what limits the scope of the human mind so much, when we imagine that one and the same person is hardly ever capable of studying a number of sciences; that in order to be good at physics or medicine, one must be inept in rhetoric or theology, and that there must be as many different kinds of skill as there are distinct disciplines.

This idea derives, on the one hand, from the fact that people often confuse nature and custom by considering the aptitude of some people for one science rather than another as an effect of their natural make-up rather than — as is often the case — a purely chance inclination which results from necessity, education or habit. On the other hand, it comes from failing to notice that there is properly only one science in the world, which is the science of ourselves, and that all the other sciences are only special applications of this.

In fact, the difficulty one finds today in learning languages, morals, and everything else comes from not knowing how to relate them to this general science. Thus it may happen that those who accept that women are capable of doing physics or medicine might think, despite that, that they are not also capable of those things which we are about to discuss. However, there is the same problem with both objections; what is at issue is clear thinking. One thinks properly when one applies one's mind seriously to the objects which present themselves, in order to get clear and distinct ideas of them, to consider them from every angle and in all their relations, and not to make any judgements about them except those which seem to be manifestly true. In order to have a perfect science all one has to do is arrange one's thoughts in a natural order. That involves nothing which is beyond the capacity of women; and those women who are educated by this method in physics or medicine will be able to make progress in a similar way in all the other sciences.

Women are capable of grammar

Why could women not recognise that, since we are obliged by the necessity of living in society to communicate our thoughts by some external signs, the most appropriate way to do so is by speaking, which consists in using words which are suitable for human beings; that there must be as many words available as there are ideas to be expressed; that there should be some connection between the sound and meaning of words, so that they can be more easily learned and remembered and we do not have to increase the number of words to infinity; that we have to arrange words in the most natural order and the order which is closest to the order of our ideas, and that we should use only as many words in our discourses as we need in order to make ourselves understood.

These reflections would put any woman in a position to work as an academician towards the perfection of her mother language, reforming or deleting inappropriate words, introducing new words, regulating word-usage according to reason and an accurate knowledge of languages. The method by which she learned her native language would be sufficient to learn a foreign language, to decipher its fine details, to read authors in that language and thereby to become very skilled at grammar and in what are called the humanities.

Rhetoric

Women, just as much as men, speak only in order to get across their point of view and to make others inclined to act as they would wish, which is called persuasion. They succeed naturally in this better than we do. And in order to do so in an artful way, they would only need to learn how to present things as they appear to them or as they would appear to those whom they wish to persuade. Since all human beings are created in the same way, they are almost always affected in the same way by objects; if there are any variations in this regard, they derive from their inclinations, their habits or their condition. This is something which a woman could find out with a little reflection and practice; and, knowing now to arrange her ideas in the most appropriate way, to express them with grace and politeness and to adjust her gestures, facial expression and her voice appropriately, she would possess true eloquence.

Morality

It is not credible that women could practise virtue to such a high degree without being able to penetrate to its basic maxims. In fact, a woman who is already educated in the way I have outlined would discover the rules of conduct for herself by discovering the three kinds of obligations which include the whole of morality, the first of which refer to God, the second to ourselves and the third to our neighbour. The clear and distinct ideas she would have formed of her mind and of the union of body and soul would have led her infallibly to recognise that there exists another infinite spirit, the author of the whole of nature, and she would acquire those feelings towards him which are the basis of religion. Having learned in physics what constitutes the pleasure of the senses, and the way in which external objects contribute towards the perfection of the mind and the preservation of the body, she would not fail to see that one would have to be one's own enemy not to use the pleasures of sense with a great deal of moderation. Then if she subsequently thought about herself as involved in civil society with other people like herself, subject to the same passions and to needs which could be satisfied only by mutual assistance, she would accept without difficulty the idea on which all our system of justice depends, namely, that one should treat others as one would wish to be treated oneself and, for this reason, that one should control one's desires, the lack of control of which, called cupidity, causes all of life's problems and evils.

Law and politics

She would become even more convinced of the last one of these duties if she pressed on further and discovered the foundation of politics and jurisprudence. Since both of these sciences are concerned only with the duties of human beings to each other she would see that, in order to know one's obligations in civil society, it is necessary to know what persuaded people to establish it in the first place. She would therefore imagine human beings as if they were outside civil society, where she would find that they are all completely free and equal, with nothing more than a tendency to self-preservation and an equal right to everything which is necessary for self-preservation. But she would notice that this equality would involve them in a war or permanent state of distrust which would be contrary to their objective, and the natural light of reason would dictate that they could not live together in peace unless everyone surrendered his rights and made contracts or conventions; that in order to validate such contracts and overcome their anxiety, they would have to have recourse to a third party who, by assuming authority, would force each individual to observe what he had promised to the others. Since this person is chosen exclusively for the benefit of his subjects, he should have no other objective; and to achieve the purpose for which he was established, he would have to be lord of property and of people, of war and of peace.

In examining this issue in depth, what would prevent a woman from finding out what is meant by natural justice? What would prevent her from discovering what a contract is, or what is meant by authority and obedience; what is the nature of law, and what penalties should be used; what is civil law and the law of nations, what are the duties of a prince and of his subjects? In a word, she would understand from her own reflections and from her books anything which is necessary in order to be a lawyer or a politician.

Geography

Having acquired a perfect knowledge of herself and been instructed well in the general rules of human conduct, she would find no difficulty in learning how people live in other countries. Since she would have observed that variations in weather, seasons, place, age, diet, company and exercise cause changes and different passions in herself, she would have no difficulty in realising that these variations produce the same effects in the case of entire populations; that different peoples have different inclinations, customs, mores and laws depending on their distance from the sea, from the north or the south, or depending on whether they have plains, mountains, rivers or forests in their countries, whether the land is more or less fertile and produces characteristic types of food, and depending on the trade and business they conduct with people near and far. She could study all these things and thereby learn about the customs, wealth, religion, government and concerns of twenty or thirty different nations just as easily as if they were so many individual families. For, as regards the location of kingdoms, the effect of the sea and of lands, of islands and of continents, there is no more difficulty in understanding these things from a map than in understanding the sections and streets of a town and the roadways of the province in which one lives.

Origin of the diversity of customs among different peoples

Secular history

Knowledge of the present could give her the desire to know the past as well. What she has learned from geography would also be a great help in this endeavour, giving her a way of understanding matters such as wars, travel, or negotiations by indicating the places where they took place, the routes, paths and boundaries between states. What she knows about the way in which human beings generally behave from reflections she has made on herself, would enable her to understand politics and to understand interests and passions. It would help her to understand the complexity of undertakings and the source of revolutions, and to supplement large-scale plans with the little details which made them succeed and which have escaped historians. As a result of the accurate ideas which she has of vice and virtue, she would notice the flattery, passions, and ignorance of authors and would thereby protect herself from the corruption to which one is exposed in reading histories where these faults are usually found. Just as ancient politics was not as subtle as its modern equivalent, and just as the interests of princes were less interconnected in former times than at present and commerce was less widespread, it requires more intelligence to understand and disentangle the gazettes than Livy or Quintus Curtius.[28]

Church history and theology

There are many people who find church history more attractive and more substantive than secular or civil history, because they notice that it challenges reason and virtue more, and that passions and prejudices camouflaged in the name of religion help the mind to understand something which is very characteristic of its conduct. A woman would apply herself to this with greater dedication in proportion to her evaluation of its importance. She would be convinced that the books of Scripture are no less authentic than any other books we have; that they contain the true religion and all the principles on which it is based; that the New Testament, in which the history of Christianity properly begins, is no more difficult to understand than the Greek and Latin authors, and that those who read it with childlike simplicity, seeking only the kingdom of God, will discover its truth and meaning with greater facility and pleasure than that of enigmas, emblems or fables. Having directed her own mind by the morality of Jesus Christ, she would be capable of directing others, curing them of their scruples and resolving their crises of conscience more soundly than if she had filled her head with all the casuists in the world.

I cannot see why, in the course of her studies, she could not notice as easily as a man how the Gospel was passed from person to person, from one kingdom to another, and from one century to another down to our own time; nor why she would not acquire the idea of the true theology from reading the Fathers of the church and understand that it consists only in knowing the history of Christians and the individual thoughts of those who wrote about them. In this way she would become competent enough to write books on religion, to teach the truth and combat novelties by showing what has always been believed in the whole church concerning any questions which are disputed.

Civil law

If a woman is able to learn from history the nature of all civil societies, how they were formed, and how they survive because of a fixed and stable authority which is exercised by magistrates and various officers who are subject one to another, then she would be no less capable of learning the application of this authority in laws, ordinances and regulations which are designed for the conduct of those who are subject to it, and which apply to the relations between people according to their diverse conditions and to the possession and use of property. Is it so difficult to understand what is the relation between a husband and his wife, between a father and his children, between a master and his domestic servants, between a lord and his vassals, between those who are allies, between a tutor and his pupil? Is there such a great mystery in understanding what is involved in possessing something as a result of a purchase, exchange, donation, bequest, will, prescription, or usufruct, and what are the necessary conditions for making these practices valid?

Canon law

It does not seem as if one would need more intelligence to understand Christian society than to understand civil society, to get an accurate idea of the type of authority which is peculiar to it and on which all its conduct is based, and to distinguish precisely between the authority which Jesus Christ left to his church and the power which belongs only to temporal rulers. Having made this distinction — which is absolutely necessary in order to understand canon law properly — a woman could study canon law and notice the extent to which it is modelled on civil law and the extent to which civil and spiritual jurisdiction have become conflated. She could understand the hierarchy, the functions of prelates, and the powers of councils, popes, bishops and parish priests. She could also understand church discipline and its rules and variations; she could understand what canons, privileges and exemptions are, how benefices are established, and what is meant by using or owning them. In a word, she could understand the customs and rules of the church and the duties of all those who compose it. There is nothing in all this which a woman is not well able to learn, and thus she could become very expert in canon law.

These are a few general ideas about the most specialised kinds of knowledge which men used both to show off their intelligence and to make money, and which they have retained for such a long time at the expense of women. And although women have no less right to this knowledge than men, the latter have thought about it and acted in a way which is so unjust that there is nothing comparable to it in the use of material goods.

It was thought in the case of material goods that prescription applied for the sake of peace and the security of families; in other words, if a man enjoyed someone else's goods without hindrance and in good faith for a certain period of time, then he could remain in possession of them and no one could subsequently claim otherwise. But no one ever dared think that those who were dispossessed, by negligence or otherwise, were incapable of recovering their possessions in some other way and no one ever regarded their incapacity as anything other than a feature of civil law.

In contrast, people were not satisfied in not inviting women to participate in the sciences and in employment after a lengthy prescription against them; they went further and argued that their exclusion was based on some natural lack of ability on their part.

It is not because of any natural inability that women are excluded from the sciences

However there is nothing more illusory than this assumption. Whether one considers the sciences themselves or the organ which is used to acquire them, one finds that the two sexes are equally suited to them. There is only one single method and one way of getting the truth — which is its nourishment — into the mind, just as there is only one way of getting nourishment into any type of stomach in order to nourish the body. As regards differences in the organ which makes us more or less suited to science, if one considers the evidence in good faith, one must admit that it favours women.

Who are most suited to the sciences?

One cannot deny that, among men, those who are very gross and material are ordinarily stupid and, on the contrary, that the more delicate are always the most intelligent. I find that experience is so widespread and constant in this respect that there is no need to support it with reasons as well. Therefore, since the fair sex has a temperament more delicate than ours they would not fail, at the very least, to equal us if they applied themselves to study.

I foresee that this suggestion will not be appreciated by many people who will find it a bit exaggerated. I can see no alternative, however; some imagine that it is to the glory of our sex to put it in first place everywhere. I believe that it is a matter of justice to give everyone their due.

Both sexes have an equal right to the sciences

In fact all of us, men and women, have an equal right to the truth because everyone's mind is equally capable of discovering the truth and we are all affected in the same way by the objects which make impressions on our bodies. This right to the same knowledge which nature confers on all of us derives from the fact that we all have the same need for knowledge. There is no one who does not search for happiness, and all our actions are directed to this end. No one can do this successfully without clear and distinct knowledge. Even Jesus Christ and St Paul make us hope for knowledge because the happiness of the next life consists in this. A miser considers himself happy as long as he knows that he possesses great riches; an ambitious person is happy when he knows that he has surpassed his peers. In a word, all the happiness of human beings, genuine or imaginary, is nothing but knowledge, that is, the thought that they possess whatever they desire.

Happiness consists in knowledge

This is what makes me believe that it is only true ideas, acquired from study — which are unchanging and independent of the possession or lack of property — which can bring true happiness in this life. Thus what makes a miser incapable of being happy simply knowing that he has riches is that, in order for this knowledge to make him happy, it would have to be joined with the desire or imagination of possessing the riches only for the immediate present.[29] Therefore when he imagines being separated from his riches and their being outside his control, he cannot think about it without suffering. It is completely different in the case of the knowledge one has of oneself and of all those other truths which depend on it, especially those which are relevant to the conduct of one's life. Because both sexes, therefore, are capable of the same happiness, they both have the same right to everything which helps them to acquire such happiness.

Virtue consists in knowledge

When one says that happiness consists primarily in the knowledge of the truth, one does not exclude virtue from happiness; on the contrary, one thinks that virtue is the most essential part of happiness. However a person does not become happy by being virtuous except in so far as he knows he is virtuous or that he tries to be so. In other words, although seeing someone practise virtue is sufficient to think that he is happy even if he is not fully aware of it himself, and though this practice of virtue with a confused and imperfect knowledge can contribute to achieving happiness in the next life, it is certain that a person cannot consider himself truly happy without knowing that he does what he ought to do, just as he would not think he was rich if he did not know that he possessed riches.

Why so few people love virtue

The reason why there are so few people who have a desire and love for genuine virtue is that they are not acquainted with it and, since they are not conscious of virtue when they practise it, they do not experience the satisfaction it brings, which is the happiness about which we are speaking. This is because virtue is not a simple speculation about the good which we are obliged to seek, but an effective desire which comes from one's conviction about it; and one could not practise virtue with pleasure without feeling some emotion. It is a little like the situation where the best drinks can sometimes taste sharp or bitter if one is distracted by something else when they are on one's tongue and is not aware of their effect on the palate.

One must be wise in order to be genuinely virtuous

Both sexes need enlightenment, not only to find their happiness in the practice of virtue, but even more so in order to practise virtue. It is conviction which makes us act, and a person is all the more convinced of his duty to the extent that he knows it perfectly. The little which is said here about morals is enough to show that knowledge of ourselves is very important to strengthen our convictions about the duties to which we are obliged. And it would not be difficult to show how all the other sciences contribute to it, nor to show that the reason why so many people practise virtue so poorly or become dissolute is exclusively a lack of self-knowledge.

Why are some learned people not virtuous

The reason why people commonly believe that it is not necessary to be wise in order to be virtuous, is that they see a number of people who are not virtuous and who otherwise pass for well-educated. People conclude from this that, not only is knowledge useless for virtue, but that it is often a hindrance to it. This mistake makes most of those who have a reputation for being more enlightened than others suspect in the eyes of weaker and less educated minds and, at the same time, it gives these people a distrust and aversion for the highest science.

This does not take into account the fact that it is only false learning which allows people, or perhaps even forces them, into a dissolute life. The confused ideas of ourselves and of the various factors involved in our actions, which are suggested by false philosophy, disturb the mind so much that it does not know itself, the things in its environment or their relation to itself and is incapable of coping with the weight of the difficulties with which it is faced in this obscurity; as a result it is forced to succumb and abandon itself to its passions, because reason is too weak to prevent it from doing so.

Study would not make women proud

The strange idea which common folk have, that study would make women more evil and proud, is based only on an unreasonable fear. Only a false science would be able to produce such an evil result. One cannot learn true science without becoming more humble; to appreciate one's weakness all one has to do is consider all the details of the machine [of the body]: the subtlety of its organs, the almost infinite number of its movements, and the painful irregularities to which it is so often subject. There is no study more capable of inspiring humility, moderation and gentleness in any type of man than examining, by studying physics, the link between his mind and his body and noticing that the mind is subject to so many needs; it is so dependent in its operations on the most delicate parts of the body that it is constantly exposed to a thousand kinds of disturbance and unpleasant experiences. Thus, no matter what knowledge one acquires, it takes very little to confuse the mind completely; a little bile or blood which is warmer or colder than usual might throw it into a fit, into madness or anger, and cause it to suffer terrible convulsions.

Since these considerations apply to a woman's mind just as much as to a man's, they would rid her mind of pride much more than they would introduce it. Having filled her mind with the best knowledge available, if a woman recalled all her previous conduct to see how she achieved the happy condition which she enjoyed, she would find a reason for being even more humble rather than for exalting herself above others. For she would be bound to see, in this review, that she previously had an untold number of prejudices from which she could not free herself except by fighting strenuously against the effects of custom, example, and the passions which controlled her despite her efforts; that all the efforts she made to discover the truth were almost completely useless and that it was only by chance that she discovered the truth when she thought least about it, in circumstances which occur hardly once in a lifetime and to very few people. She would conclude infallibly from this that it is unjust and ridiculous to resent or despise those who are less enlightened than oneself or who hold a different opinion, and that one should rather have more understanding and compassion for them. If others do not see the truth as we do, it is not their fault. Rather it is because the truth was not apparent to them when they searched for it, and because there is still some kind of veil on them or on us which prevents the truth from appearing to their minds in its full brilliance. When a woman considers that she accepts as true what she would have formerly thought was false, she would doubtless see that she could subsequently make new discoveries as a result of which she would consider false or erroneous what had previously seemed to be very true.

Very important advice for the learned

If there were any women who became proud after being educated, there are also some men who fall daily into the same vice; it should not be understood as an effect of the knowledge which they possess, but of the fact that people made a mystery of it for their sex. Since, on the one hand, these types of knowledge are usually very confused and, on the other hand, those who acquire them see them as a benefit which is peculiar to themselves, one should not be surprised if they took them as a reason for boasting. It is almost inevitable that the same thing happens in this situation as to those who, having few possessions and a lowly birth, make a great fortune by hard work. When they see themselves raised to a position which those of their class were not used to reaching, a spirit of dizziness takes hold of them and makes things appear very different to the way they are. At least it is very probable that the alleged pride of educated women is nothing in comparison with the pride of those educated men who claim the title of master or wise man; women would be less subject to this pride if their sex joined with us in an equal share of the benefits which cause it.

Knowledge is necessary for other things apart from employment

It is therefore a common mistake to imagine that study is useless for women because, it is said, they do not have any of the offices for which one studies. Study is just as necessary for them as well-being and virtue because, without it, one cannot possess perfectly either of these latter. It is necessary in order to acquire precision in thought and in action; it is necessary so that we can know ourselves and the things which surround us, that we can use them properly and regulate our passions by moderating our desires. One of the uses of science is to make oneself competent to assume offices or responsibilities, and one needs to learn as much as one can in order to become a judge or a bishop, because otherwise one could not perform the functions of these offices properly; but one should not study in order to achieve these offices and thereby to become happy in the enjoyment of the honours and benefits which result from them, for that would be to make a sordid and base use of the sciences.

Thus it is only a lack of understanding or a secret and blind prejudice which makes people say that women should remain excluded from the sciences because they have never publicly had a part in them. The goods of the mind are not like those of the body; they are not subject to prescription and no matter how long one has been deprived of them, it is always right to recover them. Since the same physical goods cannot be possessed at the same time by many people without diminishing the share of each one, there was good reason to protect families by defending — to the detriment of prior owners — the claim of those who were in possession of something in good faith [as a result of prescription].

There is no prescription in scientific matters

However it is completely different with respect to the benefits of the mind. Everyone has a right to everything which results from sound judgement. The province of reason is boundless; it has an equal jurisdiction in every person. We are all born judges of those things which affect us; and if it is not possible for all of us to dispose of these things with equal power, we can at least all know them equally well. Just as everyone enjoys the use of light and air without this sharing being to the detriment of anyone, likewise everyone could possess the truth without causing any harm to others. The more the truth is known, the more beautiful and luminous it appears; the more people who search for the truth, the sooner it is discovered; if both sexes had worked at it equally, they would have found it sooner. In this way truth and science are imprescriptible goods. Those who have been deprived of them can recover them without causing any loss to those who are already in possession. Therefore it can only be those who wish to dominate other minds by credulity who might have reason to fear anything from this recovery; they fear that if the sciences became so common, the glory which goes with them would also become common and the glory to which they themselves aspire would be diminished in sharing it with others.

Women are no less capable than men of civil offices

That is why there is no objection to women applying themselves to study as we do. They can make very good use of study and derive from it the two benefits which one can hope for: one, to have the clear and distinct knowledge which we naturally desire, the desire of which is sometimes smothered and annihilated by confused ideas or by the needs and distractions of daily life. The other benefit is using this knowledge as a guide for one's own conduct and for that of others in the various social classes to which people belong. This view does not tally with common opinion. There are many who would accept that women could learn whatever belongs to the physical or natural sciences; but they would not accept that they are just as capable as men in what could be called the moral sciences, for example, ethics, jurisprudence and politics and that, even if they were able to use the maxims of the moral sciences to guide their own conduct, they would still not be able to guide others.

People believe this because they do not realise that the mind needs, in all its actions, nothing more than discernment and accuracy, and that anyone who has once had these qualities in a particular science can have them equally easily and in the same way in all the others. Ethics and the moral sciences do not change the nature of our actions, which always remain physical. Morality is nothing more than knowing the way in which men interpret the actions of others in the light of their ideas of good and evil, of vice and virtue, of justice and injustice. Just as, having once understood the laws of motion in physics, one can apply them to all the changes and all the variations which occur in nature; in the same way, once one knows the true principles of the moral sciences, there is no further difficulty in applying them to new cases as they arise.

Those who have occupations are not always more intelligent than others, just because they happen to have been luckier; it does not even follow that they are more intelligent than the average person, although one would hope that only those who are most capable are employed in various offices. We always act in the same way and according to the same rules no matter what profession we have; however, the more important the profession, the wider the scope of our care and vision because we have greater responsibilities. The change which occurs in someone who is put in charge of others is similar to what happens to someone who, by going to the top of a tower, extends his vision further and discovers more things than those who remained at the base of the tower. For that reason, if women are just as capable as we are of guiding their own actions, they are also equally capable of guiding others and of having a share in the offices and titles of public life.

They are able to teach

The most simple and natural use which can be made in public of the sciences one has learned is to teach them to others. If women had studied in universities with men or in universities which are specially established for them, they could take their degrees and gain the title of doctor or master in theology or medicine, in canon or civil law. The talents which dispose them so favourably for learning would incline them to teach successfully. They would find methods and suggestive approaches for teaching their subject; they would identify skilfully the strong and weak students in order to adjust to their capacities; and the facility they have for expressing themselves, which is one of the most important abilities of a good teacher, would make them admirable teachers.

They are capable of assuming ecclesiastical offices

The profession which comes closest to a teacher's is that of a pastor or minister in the church, and no one can show that there is anything apart from custom which precludes women from it. They have a mind just like ours, capable of knowing and loving God and thus of leading others to know and love him. They have the same faith as we do. The Gospel and its promises are directed equally to men and women. The obligations of charity apply to them too, and since they know how to perform charitable actions, could they not also publicly teach the maxims of charity? Whoever can preach by his example could also, *a fortiori*, preach by his words; and a woman who would add natural eloquence to the morality of Jesus Christ would be just as capable as anyone else of exhorting, directing, and correcting others, of admitting those who are worthy into the Christian community and of expelling those who refuse to observe its rules after having submitted themselves to them. If men were used to seeing women presiding in a chair, they would be no more disturbed by it than women are currently by seeing men in the same role.

They can exercise authority

We are assembled in society only in order to live in peace and to find everything which is necessary for the body and soul by mutual help. We could not enjoy these benefits without dissension if there were no authority; in other words, to realise our goal we must have some people with power to make laws and impose penalties on those who break the laws. To use this authority properly, we must know what it requires us to do and we must be convinced that those who exercise it should not have any other objective in using it apart from realising the welfare and benefit of those who are their subjects. Since women are no less subject to this conviction than men, could men not subject themselves to women and agree not only not to resist their commands, but even to contribute as much as possible to compel those who cause problems in such an arrangement to obey also?

Women can be queens

Thus there is nothing to prevent a woman being on a throne and, in order to govern her peoples, from studying their native way of life, their concerns, laws, customs and practices; from considering nothing other than merit in distributing offices; from appointing only those who are suitable to offices in the army and the judiciary, and only enlightened and exemplary people to high offices in the church. Is it such a difficult thing that a woman could not get to know the strengths and weaknesses of a state and of those which surround it, that she could not maintain secret intelligence among foreigners in order to discover their plans and frustrate their strategies, and have spies and faithful emissaries in all suspicious places in order to become fully informed about everything that occurs there which might interest her? Is it necessary, in order to rule a kingdom, to have more dedication and vigilance than women have in their families or religious women in their convents? Would they lack subtlety in public negotiations any more than in private business; and since dutifulness and sweetness are natural to their sex, their rule would be less burdensome than in the case of many princes, and one could hope in their reign — something which one fears in many others — that the subjects would model themselves on the example of those who govern them.

It is easy to conclude that since women are capable of holding all civil authority as a sovereign, they are much more capable of being its ministers and, in a similar way, of being vice-regents, governors, secretaries, state counsellors or financial comptrollers.

They can be army generals

As far as I am concerned, I would not be more surprised to see a woman with a helmet rather than a crown on her head, presiding in a council of war rather than in a council of state; exercising her soldiers in person, arraying an army in battle and dividing it into a number of divisions, rather than enjoying seeing it done for her. Military art is no more difficult than other arts of which women are capable, except that it is more rugged and that it makes more noise and causes more harm. All one needs are eyes in order to see all the roads in a country on a reasonably good map, to see the good and poor pathways, the best places for surprise attacks or for an encampment. There are hardly any soldiers who do not know that one should occupy narrow passes before sending one's troops through them, or that one should make all one's plans on the basis of reliable information from good spies; that one should even deceive one's own army by ruses and countermarches in order better to conceal one's plans. A woman could do that, and could invent strategies to surprise the enemy and have the wind, the dust and the sun in his face, to attack him on one side and surround him from the other side; she could send him false alarms, and draw him into an ambush by a simulated retreat, give battle and be first through the breach to encourage the soldiers. Persuasion and passion are all important; women show no less ardour and determination when their honour is at stake, than is required to attack or defend a place.

They are capable of the duties of judges

What reasonable objection could there be if an educated woman of sound judgement presided at the head of a court [30] or of any other meeting? There are some able people who would have less difficulty in learning the laws and customs of a state than those of the games which women understand so well; it is as difficult to remember all these as it is to remember a whole novel. Is it not possible to see the point of a legal case just as easily as the conclusion of a plot in a play, and give as accurate a report of a trial as the story of a comedy? All these things are equally easy for those who apply themselves equally to them.

Since there is no office or profession in society which is not included among those which we have just spoken about, nor any in which one needs more knowledge or more intelligence, one must conclude that women are suited to all of them.

Apart from the natural dispositions of the body and one's ideas about the functions and duties of one's work, there is one other factor which makes a person more or less capable of performing his duties well: one's conviction about what one is obliged to do, considerations of religion and of interest, emulation among peers, the desire to gain glory and to make, maintain or increase one's fortune. A man acts differently in so far as he is more or less influenced by these things; since women are no less sensitive to them than men, they are equal to men in everything as far as work is concerned.

Women should devote themselves to study

One can therefore confidently encourage women to apply themselves to study without paying any attention to the trivial objections of those who try to divert them from it. Since women have an intellect just like ours, capable of knowing the truth which is the only thing which could occupy them worthily, they should try to avoid the reproach of hiding talents which they could have developed and of holding back the truth in idleness and indolence. There is no other way for them to protect themselves from the error and amazement to which people are so exposed who learn only by using gazettes, that is, by relying on other people's reports. Nor is there any other way of being happy in this life than by knowingly practising virtue.

The usefulness of study for women

Whatever objectives women strive for apart from living a happy life, they will achieve them through study. If the informal study circles were transformed into academies, their meetings would be more substantive, more pleasant and better attended.[31] Every woman would see the satisfaction which is possible in speaking about the most interesting things, from what she experiences sometimes in hearing others speak about them. However superficial the topics of conversation may be, they would have an opportunity of treating them in a more intellectual way than usual; and the refined manners which are so characteristic of their sex, being strengthened by solid reasoning, would improve their discussions.

Those who merely wish to please would find study a great advantage; the impact of physical beauty, enhanced by that of the mind, would be a hundred times more striking. Since women who are less beautiful are always admired when they are intelligent, the benefits of a mind cultivated by study would give them a way of compensating abundantly for what nature or fate had denied them. They would take part in the meetings of the learned and prevail over them on two counts. They would become involved in business; husbands could not avoid handing over to them the running of the family and taking their advice about everything. And if conditions were such that they could no longer be admitted to employment, they could at least know the duties of those offices and judge whether they are carried out properly by others.

The difficulties in getting as far as this should not dismay us. They are not as great as they are made out to be. The reason why people think it is so difficult to acquire certain kinds of knowledge is that most of those who aspire to doing so are taught a number of things which are completely useless. Since the whole of knowledge up to now has been almost nothing but learning the beliefs of our predecessors, and since men have given in too much to custom and the credibility of their teachers, very few have been lucky enough to discover the natural method. However one could use the natural method and show that people can become competent in much less time and with much more enjoyment than one might think.

That women have a disposition which is favourable to the sciences, and that the correct ideas of perfection, nobility and of propriety apply to them just as much as to men

Up to this point we have only considered the heads of

women and we have seen that, when considered in a general way, this part [of a woman's body] has the same relation to all the sciences, of which it is the organ, as in the case of men. However, because this organ is not exactly the same in everyone even in the case of men, and since there are some in whom the head is more suitable for some things than for others, it is necessary to go into greater detail to see if there is anything in women which makes them less suited to the sciences.

One can see that they have a more joyful and more noble face than us, they have a high, noble and broad forehead which is normally a sign of intelligent and imaginative people. One finds, in fact, that women are very vivacious, with a good imagination and memory; that means that their brain is so disposed that it receives impressions from objects easily, including impressions which are weaker or quicker and which escape those of a different disposition, and that they store these impressions and present them to the mind at the time when they are needed.[32]

Women are imaginative and intelligent

Since this disposition is accompanied by heat, it causes the mind to be affected by objects in a more lively way and to apply itself to these impressions, to penetrate them to a greater extent, and to create images from them as it pleases. Thus those who have more imagination, considering things more quickly from a greater number of perspectives, are very ingenious and creative, and discover more from one perception than many others do after a lengthy observation. They are able to represent things in a pleasant and attractive way and to identify suitable strategies and expedients quickly. They express themselves with ease and grace, and facilitate the birth of their ideas.

All this can be seen in women, and I see nothing in this disposition which is incompatible with a good mind. Discernment and accuracy are part of their natural make-up; to acquire these qualities, one must become a little bit sedentary and concentrate on things in order to avoid mistakes and errors which one makes in flitting about. It is true that the multiplicity of ideas in creative people sometimes carries their imagination away; but it is also true that one can control it by practice. We have experience of this in the greatest men of this century who are almost all very imaginative.

One could say that this temperament is the most appropriate one for society, and since human beings are not created to live alone forever and remain locked up in a study, one should in some way treasure those who have a better disposition for communicating their ideas pleasantly and usefully. Thus women, who naturally have a noble mind because of their imagination, memory and vivaciousness, can acquire the qualities of a good mind with a little study.

That is enough to show that, when we consider the head only, the two sexes are equal. There are very interesting things to be said about the rest of the body, but they only need to be mentioned in passing. Men have always had this common misfortune of, so to speak, spreading their passions all over nature. There are hardly any ideas which they have not linked with some feeling of love or hate, praise or scorn; those ideas which concern the distinction of the sexes are so gross and so clouded with feelings of imperfection, vulgarity, indecency and other nonsense that, since they can hardly be mentioned without evoking some passion or influencing the flesh against the spirit, it is often prudent to say nothing at all about them.

Nevertheless those thoughts which are unfavourable to women and which are used by small-minded people to humiliate them are based on precisely this strange mixture of confused ideas. The best compromise between the need to explain oneself and the problems of doing so with impunity, is to explain what we should understand reasonably by perfection and imperfection, by nobility and vulgarity, by decency and indecency.

Ideas of perfection and imperfection

When I think about God's existence, I understand easily that everything depends on him. When I consider the natural and internal condition of creatures (which for bodies consists in the disposition of their parts in relation to each other) and their external condition (which is their capacity for affecting or being affected by other bodies in their environment), and if I look for an explanation of these two conditions, I find none other than the will of their creator. Then I notice that bodies normally have a certain disposition which makes them capable of producing and receiving various effects, for example, that man can hear the ideas of his fellow men by means of the ears and that he can make his ideas understood by using his voice. I notice that bodies are incapable of these effects, as long as they are disposed in a different way. From this I form two ideas, one of which represents the original condition of things and all its necessary consequences, and I call this the state of perfection; and the other idea represents the opposite state, which I call imperfection.

Thus a man is perfect in my view as long as he has anything which, according to God's creation, is necessary to produce or receive the effects for which he is destined. And he is imperfect when he has more or fewer parts than are necessary, or some indisposition which impedes him from realising his destiny. That is why, since he was created in such a way that he needs nourishment in order to survive, I do not think of this need as an imperfection, no more than the necessity resulting from the use of nourishment to excrete from the body what is left over from the food.

One should not confuse perfection with nobility. These are two very different things. Two creatures could be equal in perfection but unequal in nobility.

In reflecting on myself, it seems to me that since my mind alone is capable of knowledge, it should be preferred to the body and considered as more noble. But when I consider bodies without any regard to myself, that is without thinking that they might be useful or injurious or pleasant or unpleasant for me, I cannot believe that one is more noble than the other since none of them is anything but matter arranged in different ways. Whereas if I think of myself among bodies and consider the good or evil which they can cause me, I begin to evaluate them in a different way. Thus my head considered disinterestedly does not impress me any more than the other parts of my body, but I value it more than all the other parts when I begin to think that it is of greater significance for me in the union of my mind with the body.

It is for the same reason that, although all parts of the body are equally perfect, we look on them in different ways. Even those parts of the body which we have most need of are often considered with a certain amount of contempt and aversion, because their use is less pleasant or something like that. It is the same for everything in our environment which affects us, for what makes something please one person and displease another is that it strikes them differently.

The idea of propriety[33]

The involvement of people in society is what produces the idea of propriety in them. Thus although there is neither imperfection nor lack of nobility in relieving the body, and even though this is a necessary and unavoidable consequence of its natural disposition and all ways of doing so are equal, there are some nevertheless which are considered as less decent because they cause more shock to people who witness them.[34]

Since all creatures and all their actions are equally perfect and noble when considered in themselves, without reference to the use we make of them or the respect we have for them, they are also all equally respectable when considered in the same way. For that reason one could say that what appears to be decent or indecent is almost always a result of human imagination or caprice. This can be seen in the fact that something which is respectable in one country is not so in another or in the same kingdom in different periods; and even during the same period, among people of different social classes, conditions or moods, the very same action sometimes conforms and sometimes fails to conform with decency. That is why decency is nothing more than our way of using natural things, according to the value which human beings attribute to them; and it is prudent to conform with this.

We are all so convinced of this idea even when not reflecting on it that people who — whether for reasons of respect or because they are sensitive or discreet — subject themselves in public along with common folk to the demands of propriety, in private release themselves from these demands as if they were importunate and strange burdens.

It is the same with nobility. In some provinces of India the labourers have the same rank as nobles have in our country. In some countries, they prefer soldiers to lawyers, whereas in others they do the exact opposite. Everyone judges these professions according to his own inclination towards them, or in so far as he thinks they are more or less important.

By comparing these ideas with the thoughts of common folk about women, one can see the latter's mistake without any difficulty.

The origin of the difference between the sexes. How far does it extend? That it makes no difference between men and women in respect of virtues and vices; and that, in general, temperament is neither good nor evil in itself

Origin of the difference between the sexes

Because God wished to create human beings in such a way that their coming into being depends on intercourse between two people, he designed two different bodies for this purpose. Each one was perfect in its own right and they were supposed to be as we see them today. Everything which results from the special structure of each type of body should be considered as part of its perfection. There is no reason therefore for some people to imagine that women are not as perfect as men, and to consider as a defect in women anything which is an essential feature of their sex and without which their sex would be useless for the purpose for which it was created; that purpose is completely defined in terms of fecundity, and is destined for the most important function in the world, namely, to conceive us and nourish us in their wombs.

Women contribute more than men to generation[35]

Both sexes are necessary in order to produce together another human being. If we understood how much our sex [i.e. men] contributes to conception, we would have discovered plenty for us to be displeased about. It is difficult to understand on what basis some people think that men are more noble than women in matters regarding children. It is clearly the women who conceive us and form us, who give us life, birth and education. It is true that this causes them a lot more bother than it does us; however their toil should not be to their disadvantage, nor should it earn them contempt instead of the esteem which they deserve. Who would want to say that the fathers and mothers who work at rearing their children, the good princes who govern their subjects, and the magistrates who dispense justice, are less worthy of respect than those whose mediation and help they use to perform their duties?

On temperament

There are medical doctors who said a lot about the temperament of the sexes to the detriment of women, who have given discourses at great length to show that women must have a temperament which is completely different to ours and which makes them inferior in everything. However, their reasons are only feeble conjectures which occur to the minds of those who judge things on the basis of appearances and prejudices.

Seeing the two sexes differentiated more by their civil roles than by those which are characteristic of them, they imagined that that was how things ought to be; and not distingushing carefully enough what derives from custom and education from what is due to nature, they attributed to one and the same cause everything which they observed in society, because they thought that God, in making man and woman, had made them in a way which would produce all the differences which we observe between them.

That is to carry the distinction between the sexes too far. One should confine the difference between the sexes to God's plan of creating human beings by the intercourse of two people, and not include anything which is not necessary for that purpose. Thus we see that men and women are similar in almost everything which pertains to the internal and external make-up of the body, and that the natural functions on which our survival depends are carried out in the same way in both of them. The only reason why there are some organs in one which are not in the other is to give birth to a third human being. It does not follow from this, as some imagine, that women have less strength and energy than men. Since we can decide this issue correctly only on the basis of experience, do we not find that there are differences between individual women just as there are between men. There are both strong and weak members in each sex. Men who were reared in idleness are often worse than women, and give up first under the burden of work; but when they are toughened by work through necessity or otherwise, they become equal and sometimes even better than others.

It is the same with women. Those who are engaged in hard work are more robust than the ladies who handle only a needle. This would suggest that if both sexes exercised equally, one could become as strong as the other. This was noticed in earlier times in another commonwealth, in which exercise and competition were common to both sexes. The same thing is reported about the Amazons in South America.

One should ignore expressions which are unfavourable to women

One should not, therefore, rely on certain common expressions which reflect the present condition of the two sexes. If someone wants mockingly to blame a man for having little courage, resolution or toughness, he is called effeminate, as if one wished to say that he is as cowardly and as soft as a woman.[36] In contrast, in order to praise a woman who is exceptionally courageous, strong, or intelligent, one says that she is like a man. These expressions, which are so favourable to men, help very much to maintain the high opinion which people have of men, because they do not realise that these expressions are only apparently true; they take both nature and custom for granted without any distinction, and hence they are completely contingent or arbitrary views. Virtue, kindness and propriety are so characteristic of women that, if their sex were not so little esteemed and if people had wished to adopt this way of speaking in our language, one would say 'he is like a woman' whenever one wished to mark with praise the fact that some man possessed these qualities to a superior degree.

However it is not physical strength which should distinguish men. Otherwise beasts would be better than men and, among men, those who are more robust would be regarded more highly. Indeed it is known from experience that those who have a lot of strength are rarely fit for anything else except manual work, and that those who have less physical strength usually have more brains. The best philosophers and the greatest princes were rather delicate, and the greatest army captains might not perhaps have wished to wrestle with their most junior soldiers. If we go into the courts, we can see if the best judges are always comparable in strength to the least of their ushers.

It is therefore useless to rely so much on bodily make-up rather than on the mind in order to explain the differences which can be seen between the two sexes.

Temperament is not an indivisible point. Just as one cannot find two people in whom it is exactly similar, so likewise one cannot identify exactly in what respect they differ. There are different kinds of choleric, sanguine, and melancholic temperaments, and none of these differences prevents one of them from being sometimes as capable as the other, nor does it preclude there being excellent men of every kind of temperament. Even assuming that the temperament of the two sexes is as dissimilar as is imagined, there is an even greater difference between many men who are considered to be equally competent. The extent of the differences [between the sexes] is so insignificant that it is only a spirit of quibbling which makes us take any notice of them.

It seems as if what so magnifies, in our thinking, the distinction which we are speaking about is that we fail to examine carefully enough those things which can be observed in women. This failure makes us fall into the mistake of those who have confused minds, who do not distinguish sufficiently what belongs to each thing and attribute to one what belongs to another because both have been found together in the same subject. That is why, when people see that women are so different in their behaviour and in their roles, they attribute these differences to their temperament because their true cause is unknown.

Women can claim superiority with respect to the body

Besides, if one wished to decide by comparing bodies which is the more excellent of the two sexes, women could claim victory without even taking account of the internal structure of their bodies and of the fact that the most interesting thing in the world takes place within them: namely, the conception of human beings, the most noble and admirable of all creatures. Who could stop them from saying that their external appearance makes them the winners, that grace and beauty are natural and characteristic of them, and that all this gives rise to effects which are as visible as they are common; and that, if what they can accomplish as a result of what is in their heads makes them at least equal to men, their external appearance hardly ever fails to make them the victors?

Since beauty is an advantage which is just as real as strength or health, we are not precluded by reason from giving it an even greater value than other qualities. If one wished to measure its value by the feelings and passions which it excites, which is the way one judges most other things, one would find that there is nothing which is more valued since there is nothing which is more effective; that is to say, there is nothing which affects and excites the passions more, which confuses them and invigorates them in a greater variety of ways than the perception of beauty.

All temperaments are almost equal

There would be no need to speak any further about the temperament of women if an author as famous as he is respectable had not decided to consider it the source of the faults which are commonly attributed to them;[37] this suggestion greatly encourages people to think that women are less worthy of respect than we are. Without reporting his opinion, I would say that in order properly to examine the temperament of both sexes with respect to vice and virtue, it would have to be examined in a neutral condition in which there was as yet neither vice nor virtue in nature. Besides, one finds that what is called virtue at one time can become a vice at another, depending on how it is used, and therefore all temperaments are equal in this respect.

What is virtue

In order to understand this idea better, one must realise that our soul alone is capable of virtue which, in general terms, consists in a firm and stable resolve to do what one thinks is best depending on various circumstances. The body is properly only the organ and instrument of this resolution, like a sword in one's hand for attack or defence. All the various dispositions which make the body more or less well suited for this function should be called neither good nor evil, except in so far as their consequences are ordinarily and to a significant extent good or evil. For example, the tendency to flee in order to avoid evils which threaten us is indifferent because there are some evils which cannot be avoided otherwise; and, indeed, it is a sign of prudence to flee. On the other hand, it is blameworthy cowardice to allow oneself to be carried away by fear whenever some evil can be overcome by a courageous resistance which results in more good than harm.

Women are no more inclined to vice than men

The mind is no less capable in women than in men of making this firm resolve which constitutes virtue and of recognising the circumstances in which it should be practised. Women can control their passions just as well as we can, and they are not more inclined to vice than to virtue. One could even tilt the balance in their favour on this issue because affection for children, which is incomparably stronger in women than in men, is naturally linked with compassion which, in turn, could be called the virtue and the bond of civil society. It is impossible to imagine that society is reasonably established for any other purpose apart from the mutual satisfaction of needs and common necessities. And if one looked closely at how passions arise in us, one would find that the way in which women treat us when we are in distress, almost like their own children, is like a natural development of their contribution to the birth and education of men.

That the differences which can be observed in the conduct of men and women derive from their education

It is all the more important to notice that the dispositions with which we are born are neither good nor evil, because otherwise one cannot avoid a rather common mistake of attributing to nature something which results only from custom.

Influence of external conditions

It is possible to worry a lot looking for a reason why we are subject to certain faults and why we have characteristic ways of behaving, because we fail to observe what habit, practice, education and our external circumstances can cause in us, in other words, the influence of our sex, age, luck, and the role which we have in society. Since it is certain that all these various factors differentiate our thoughts and passions in an infinite number of ways, they also incline minds to consider truths which are presented to them in very different ways. For this reason a single maxim proposed at the same time to commoners, soldiers, judges and princes strikes each of them differently and inclines them to act in very different ways. Since men are rarely concerned with anything apart from externals, they consider externals as the standard and guide for their opinions. Thus it happens that some of them ignore as useless something which significantly concerns others, that soldiers are shocked by something which flatters judges, and that people of the same temperament often understand in different ways things which are understood in the same way by people of very different temperaments who happen to be equally rich or to have had the same education.

This is not to claim that all men enter the world with the same bodily make-up. That would be an ill-founded assumption; there are those who are quick-witted and those who are slow, but it does not seem as if this diversity in any way prevents minds from receiving the same instruction. All it does is to cause some to receive it more quickly and more easily than others. Thus, whatever temperament women have, they are no less suited to truth and study than we are. If one finds that there is some fault or impediment in some women at present, or even that they do not all consider important things in the same way as men do — something which however is inconsistent with our experience — that should be explained completely in terms of the external conditions of their sex and the education which they receive, which includes the ignorance in which they are left, the prejudices and errors they are taught, the example which they get from other women, and all the mannerisms to which propriety, restraint, reserve, subjection and timidity reduce them.

Women's faults result from their education

What education do women get?

In fact no opportunity is missed to persuade women that the great difference which they observe between their sex and ours derives either from reason or from divine institution. Their clothing, education and training could not be more different to ours. A young girl is only secure at her mother's side or under the eyes of a governess who never leaves her alone. She is made to feel afraid of everything. She is threatened by ghosts in all those parts of the house where she might wander alone; there is something to fear even on main roads and in big churches if she is not escorted. She applies her mind exclusively to the great care which is taken in dressing her up. There are so many people looking at her and so much said about her beauty that she focuses all her ideas on that; the compliments she gets in this respect make her place all her happiness in it. Since no one talks to her about anything else, she does not think of doing anything else and does not raise her sights any higher. The most exercise that women get comes from dancing, writing, and reading; their whole library consists in a few small devotional books together with whatever fits in a little desk.

The whole of women's science is reducible to working with a needle. The mirror is her great tutor, it is the oracle which women consult. Balls, plays, and fashions are the subjects of their conversations. They rely on the salons they attend, as if they were famous academies, to get all the news about their sex. And if some of them stand out from others as a result of reading certain books — and they would have a fair amount of difficulty in getting their hands on these in order to open up their minds — they are often forced to conceal it. Most of their companions, because of jealousy or for some other reason, never miss a chance of accusing them of affectation.

A mind is even more useless in the case of lower-class girls who are forced to earn a living by working. Someone takes care to teach them a skill which is appropriate to their sex as soon as they are able to learn, and the necessity of working without interruption prevents them from thinking of anything else. As soon as either one or the other type of girl is reared in this way and reaches a marriageable age, they either get married or they are locked up in a convent where they continue to live as they had up to that point.

Is there anything in what women are taught which helps give them a solid education? It seems on the contrary that their education has been designed to diminish their courage, obscure their minds and fill them with nothing but vanity and foolishness, to smother all the seeds of virtue and of truth in them, to undermine all the dispositions toward great things which they might have, and to deprive them of any desire of improving themselves (like us) by removing the means of doing so.

When I think about the ways in which men consider what they regard as faults in women, I find that there is something in this way of going on which is unworthy of rational people. If there is something equally wrong in both sexes, then the one which accuses the other sins against natural justice. If there is more to criticise in men and if we do not notice it, we are rash to speak of the faults of the other sex. If we see our own faults and say nothing about them, we are unjust in blaming the other sex which has fewer faults. If there is more good in women than in men, then men should be accused either of ignorance or of envy in not acknowledging it. When there is more virtue than vice in someone, the former should provide an excuse for the latter; and whenever a woman has faults which are incorrigible, and when the means of ridding herself of them or protecting herself against them are lacking as they are in the case of women, then she deserves compassion rather than contempt. Finally, if the faults in question are trivial or only apparent, it is indiscreet or malicious to pay any attention to them, and it is easy to show that this is what is commonly done in the case of women.[38]

The faults attributed to women are imaginary

Timidity

Women are said to be timid and incapable of defending themselves. People say that they are afraid of their own shadow, that a baby's cry terrifies them and that the sound of the wind makes them tremble. This is not generally true. There are many women who are as fearless as men, and we know that the most timid often make a virtue of necessity. Timidity is almost inseparable from virtue, and all good people are timid; it takes very little to make virtuous people afraid because they do not want to harm anyone and they realise how widespread evil is among men. This is a natural passion from which no one is exempt. Everyone fears death and life's infirmities, the most powerful princes fear a revolt of their subjects or an invasion by their enemies, and the most valiant captain fears being taken by surprise in battle.

A person fears more or less in proportion to whether or not he believes he has the strength to resist. Fear is only blameworthy in those who are strong enough to overcome whatever threatens them. It would be just as unreasonable to accuse of cowardice a judge or a scholar who had never thought of anything but study, because they refuse to engage in a duel, as it would be to accuse of cowardice a soldier who had always borne arms, because he was unwilling to become involved in a dispute with a learned philosopher.

Women are reared in such a way that they have reason to fear everything. They have no education with which to cope with problems in intellectual matters. They are excluded from the training which would give them skill and strength for attack or defence. They see themselves exposed to suffer with impunity the abuse of a sex which is so subject to fits of passion, which looks down on them with contempt, and which often treats other people with more cruelty and anger than wolves treat each other.

That is why timidity should not be considered a defect in women, but rather a reasonable passion to which they owe the modesty which is so characteristic of them and the two greatest advantages of life, an inclination to virtue and an aversion to vice, which the majority of men fail to acquire despite all the education and teaching they get.

Avarice

The fear of being without property is the usual cause of avarice. Men are no less subject to avarice than women; if one were to take count, I suspect that the number of men would turn out to be higher than the number of women and their avarice would be more blameworthy. Since there is a short distance between any two vices and whatever virtue is the mean between them,[39] people often think that a virtue is a vice and they confuse avarice with a praiseworthy thrift.

Since the same action can be good when performed by one person and bad when performed by another, it often happens that what is evil is us is not at all evil in women. They are deprived of every opportunity to make a living by using their intellects because they are denied access to the sciences and to employment. Therefore since they are not as well placed as men to protect themselves against the misfortunes and infirmities of life, they are likely to be more affected by them. Thus one should not be surprised that, since they have to work so hard to acquire so few goods, they take so much care to protect them.

Credulity

If women accept very easily what they are told, this results from their simplicity which prevents them from believing that those who are in authority over them are either ignorant or biased. One sins against justice by accusing them of credulity because men are even more credulous. The most able men allow themselves to be deluded too much by false appearances. Their whole science is often nothing more than a shallow credulity which, however, is a bit more extensive than that of women. I would say that they are no wiser than others except in the sense that they have believed a greater number of things more easily, and they have retained ideas of these things, such as they are, as a result of constantly reconsidering them.

Superstition

Whatever causes timidity in women is what produces the superstition which even the learned attribute to them. However it seems that, in this case, the learned are like those people who are most mistaken about something but convince themselves that they are more correct because they shout louder than others. The learned imagine that they are exempt from superstition because they notice it in a few less educated women, whereas they themselves are pitifully up to their eyes in it.

Even if all men were genuine adorers of God, in spirit and in truth, and if women always worshipped Him superstitiously, women would be excusable. They are not taught to discover God for themselves; they only know what they are told. Since the majority of men speak of God in a way which is unworthy of him and since they only distinguish him from creatures by the fact that he is their creator, one should not be surprised if women, knowing God only from the reports of men, adore him in their religion with the same sentiments which they have towards men, whom they fear and revere.

Chatter

There are people who think they can properly humiliate women by saying that they are all nothing but chatterboxes. Women have good reason to take offence at such an impertinent reproach. Their body is fortunately so disposed by their characteristic temperament that they preserve distinctly the impressions which they receive from objects; they imagine these objects without difficulty, and they express themselves with an admirable facility. That means that, since the ideas they have are activated on the slightest stimulation, they begin and continue a conversation as they wish. Since their intellectual perspicacity enables them to perceive easily the relations between things, they move easily from one subject to another and in this way they can speak for a long time without letting a conversation lapse.

The gift of speech is naturally accompanied by a great desire to use it, once an opportunity arises. It is the only bond between men in society, and many find that there is no greater pleasure nor anything which is more worthy of the mind than communicating one's thoughts to others. That is why, given that women can speak easily and are reared with other women, there would be something amiss if they failed to converse. They should not therefore be taken as chatterboxes except when they speak inappropriately or when they speak about things which they do not understand — apart from situations where they are trying to understand them.

It should not be assumed that one chatters only when speaking of clothes and fashions. The babble of novelists is often more ridiculous. This heap of words piled one on the other, which means nothing in the majority of books, is a cackle which is much more foolish than that of the lowliest women. At least one could say that the conversations of women are real and intelligible, and they are not as vain as the majority of the learned who imagine that they are more clever than their neighbours because they use more words which are meaningless. If men had as good a command of language as women, it would be impossible to shut them up. Everyone talks about the things he knows about: merchants talk about their trade, philosophers about their study, and women about what they have been able to learn. They could claim that they would converse even better and more sensibly than us if they had been educated as carefully as men.

Curiosity

What bothers some people about the conversations of women is that they show a great desire to know everything. I do not understand the values of those people who do not like women to be so curious. As far as I am concerned, I think that curiosity is a good thing; I suggest only that it not become importunate.

I think of the conversations of women like those of philosophers, in which it is also allowed to talk about things of which one is ignorant, and misunderstandings occur in both of them.

It is customary for many people to treat curious people like beggars. When they are in humour for giving they are not bothered by requests, and when they wish to show off what they know they are very willing to be asked questions. Otherwise they always say that people are too curious. Since it is assumed that women should not study, men take offence if women ask to be informed about what they learn in their studies. I think highly of women because they are curious, and I feel sorry for them because they have no way of satisfying their curiosity, for they are often prevented from doing so only by the valid fear of having recourse to foolish or boorish minds, by whom they could only be mocked rather than be instructed. It seems to me that curiosity is one of the surest signs of a good mind and a greater capacity for learning. It is a beginning of knowledge, which makes us go faster and further in the path of truth. Whenever two people are affected by the same thing, and one of them looks at it

Curiosity is a sign of intelligence

indifferently while the other goes closer in order to see better, it is a sign that the latter has eyes which are more open. The mind in both sexes is equally adapted to the sciences, and the desire for knowledge which each of them may have is no more blameworthy in one sex than the other. Whenever the mind is struck by something which it sees only obscurely it seems that, by a natural right, it wishes to be more enlightened. Since ignorance is the most serious slavery one could be in, it is as unreasonable to blame someone for trying to escape from ignorance as it is to blame some unfortunate who tries to escape from a prison in which he is confined.

Fickleness

Among all the faults which are attributed to women, a fickle or unstable temperament is the one which causes most annoyance. However men are no less subject to ficklessness; but because they perceive themselves as superior, they assume they are allowed do as they wish. They assume that once a woman becomes attached to them the bond should only be indissoluble from her side, despite the fact that they are both equal and each one is involved for his or her own sake.

There would be fewer accusations of fickleness on both sides if they realised that it is natural for human beings to be so, that whoever says 'mortal' says 'changeable', and that being changeable is an unavoidable necessity because of the way in which we are made. We only judge things, we only love or hate them, on the basis of appearances which are independent of us. The same things appear differently to us, sometimes because they have undergone some change, sometimes because we ourselves have changed. The same meat gives us very different sensations depending on whether it is more or less seasoned, hot, or cold. Even if the meat remains unchanged, we would be affected by it in different ways when we are sick or healthy. We are indifferent to some things in our infancy which we consider passionately ten years later, because our bodies have changed in the meantime.

Why we should not blame others for not loving us

If someone loves us, it is because she thinks we are lovable; and if someone else hates us, it is because we seem loathsome to her. At one time we think highly of those whom we formerly despised, because they did not always appear to us in the same way, or because either they or we have changed. On some occasions we open our hearts to something, even though it would have been closed to the same thing a quarter of an hour earlier.

The contrast we often find in ourselves between two opposite feelings which one and the same object arouses in us convinces us, despite what we might wish to think, that the passions are not free and that it is unfair to complain about being thought of otherwise than one would wish. Just as little is needed to love someone, very little is needed to lose another's love, and this passion depends as little on us in its progress as in its inception. Of ten people who would like to be loved, it often happens that the one who is least deserving, who is lowest by birth and is least good-looking, will win over the others because he or she seems to be more cheerful or has some other feature which is in fashion or which suits our taste, given our condition at the time.

Cunning

If someone realised what they were saying in accusing women of being more cunning than men, far from doing them an injustice, they would in fact be speaking in their favour, because they would thereby recognise that women are also more intelligent and prudent. Cunning is a secret way of achieving one's aim without being diverted from it; one needs intelligence to discover this way and one needs skill in order to follow it. One could hardly object if someone used artifice to avoid being deceived. Knavery is much more dangerous and much more common among men; it has always been the most common way of getting those positions or offices in which one can cause most harm. And whereas men who wish to deceive use their property, their education, and their power, from which one is rarely protected, women can use only caresses and eloquence, which are natural means and against which one can more easily protect oneself whenever there is reason to guard against them.

Greater malice

To cap all the accusations and faults, it is said that women are more malicious and more evil than men. All the evil with which they can be accused is included in this idea. I do not believe that those who hold this idea imagine that there are more women than men who do evil. That would be an obvious falsehood. Women are excluded from those offices or positions, the abuse of which causes all public misfortunes; their virtue is too exemplary, while the dissolute lives of men are too well known to call them in question.

Therefore when it is alleged that women are more malicious, that could only mean that when they decide to do some evil, they do it more skilfully and they go further with it than men. Well and good. That suggests a great advantage in women. One could not be capable of a lot of evil without being very intelligent and without being, as a result, capable of much good. Women should not therefore take this reproach as more insulting than one which might be made to the rich or powerful, of being more evil than the poor because they have a greater capacity to cause harm. Women can reply that, if they are capable of causing harm, they are also capable of doing good and if the ignorance in which they are left is the reason why they are more evil than us, then knowledge by contrast would make them better.

This short discussion of the most prominent faults which are thought to be characteristic of and natural to the fair sex shows two things. One is that these faults are not as great as is commonly imagined; the other is that they can be explained by the minimal education which women are given and that, such as they are, their faults can be corrected by education; and women are no less capable of this than we are.

If philosophers had followed this rule in making up their minds about everything which pertains to women, they would have spoken more sensibly and they would not have fallen into ridiculous absurdities. But since most ancient and modern philosophers based their philosophy only on popular prejudices and were very ignorant about themselves, it is not surprising that they know so little about others. Without bothering with the ancients, one could say of modern philosophers that the way in which they are taught makes them believe, even if falsely, that they cannot improve on those who preceded them; this makes them slaves to antiquity and encourages them to adopt blindly as unchanging truths everything they find in antiquity. Because everything modern philosophers say about women is based primarily on what they have read in the ancients, it would be useful to report here some of the most unusual thoughts on this subject which have been bequeathed to us by these illustrious dead whose ashes and even whose rotten remains are so much revered today.

The opinion of Plato

Plato, the father of ancient philosophy, used to thank the gods for the three favours they had given him, but especially for the fact that he was born a man rather than a woman. If he had in mind the condition of women at that time, I would certainly agree with him. But what suggests that he had something else in mind is the doubt which he is said to have expressed often about whether or not women should be put in the same category as beasts.[40] That would be enough for reasonable people to convict him either of ignorance or stupidity, and to deprive him successfully of the claim to divinity which he no longer has except among pedants.

The opinion of Aristotle

His disciple Aristotle, for whom the glorious name 'genius of nature' is still kept in the schools because of the prejudice that he understood nature better than any other philosopher, imagined that women were nothing but monsters.[41] Who would not believe this, on the authority of such a celebrated person? To say that it is an impertinence would be to shock his supporters too overtly. If a woman, no matter how learned, had written the same about men she would lose all credibility; people would think it sufficient to refute such a stupid thing by replying that it must have been a woman or a fool who said it. Nevertheless, she would be no less correct than this philosopher. Women have been on earth just as long as men; they appear in equally large numbers and no one is surprised to meet a woman on one's travels. To be a monster, even according to the thought of this philosopher, one would have to have some extraordinary and surprising features. Women have nothing of the sort. They have always been created in the same way, always beautiful and intelligent; and if they are not made like Aristotle, they can say likewise that Aristotle was not made like them.

Those disciples of this author who lived in the time of Philo adopted a view which is no less grotesque with respect to women. They imagined on the basis of this historian's report that women were imperfect men or males. This was probably because women did not have a beard on their chins. Otherwise, I cannot understand it at all. In order for the two sexes to be perfect, they should be as we see them. If one sex resembled the other, then it would be neither one sex nor the other. If men are the fathers of women, women are the mothers of men, which makes them at least equal. One would be just as correct as these philosophers if one said that men are imperfect women!

The ridiculous opinion of Socrates

Socrates, the oracle of antiquity for morals, when speaking of the beauty of the fair sex was accustomed to compare her with a temple which looks well but is built on a sewer. One could only laugh at this idea if it did not cause offence. It seems as if he judged other people's bodies by comparison with his own, or with that of his wife who was a she-devil who caused him to hate her. He spoke of her sex in that way in order to humiliate her and because he was enraged inside himself for being as ugly as a baboon.

The thought of Diogenes

Diogenes, nicknamed 'the dog' because he only knew how to bite, seeing two women who were conversing together when passing one day, said to those in his company that they were two snakes, an aspic and a viper, who were exchanging their venoms.[42] This apophthegm* is worthy of a cultured man, and I am not surprised that it is ranked with the best philosophical sayings. If Tabarin, Verboquet and Espiègle had lived in the time of Diogenes, then we would surely find their stories more witty than his. The poor man was injured in some way and those who know him a little realise that he had nothing else to say.[43]

* i.e. a saying of an illustrious man

As regards the famous and amusing Democritus, since he liked to laugh a little, one should not take everything he said literally. He was very tall, and his wife was very short. When asked one day why they were so poorly matched, he replied jokingly in his usual manner that, when one is forced to choose and there is nothing good available, the smallest is always the best. If the same question had been put to his wife, she could have replied just as correctly that, since there is hardly anything to choose between a large and a small husband, she got hers by drawing lots because she was afraid that, had she chosen, she might have ended up with a worse one. *Democritus*

Cato, the wise and severe critic, often prayed to the gods to pardon him if he were ever so imprudent as to confide a secret to a woman. The good man had in mind a famous event in Roman history which antiquarians[†] use as a great argument to show how little discretion women have. A child of twelve years was encouraged by his mother to tell her a decision of the Senate at which he had been present and, in order to avoid her request, he made up a story that it had been decided to give every husband a number of wives. She went off immediately to tell her neighbours and to make plans with them. The whole city knew about it in half an hour. I would certainly like to know what a poor husband would do if, in a state where wives were masters as in that of the Amazons, he had been told that the Council had decided to give each wife a second husband. Surely he would say nothing at all about it! *Cato's thought*

These are some of the great and lofty thoughts which those whom the learned study like oracles have had on the subject of the fair sex. What is ludicrous and strange in all of this is that serious people take literally what the famous ancients often said in jest. It is so true that prejudices and preoccupations lead to mistakes among those very people who are accepted as the most reasonable, judicious and wise.

End

† the lovers of antiquity

Notes on the text

1 This refers to the adoption of the Copernican theory of planetary motions in the seventeenth century, primarily as a result of Galileo's influence. In France, Descartes endorsed the Copernican theory and so did all his followers, including Poulain. If we take our observations at face value, we are inclined to believe that it is the sun which moves around the earth; however, Poulain argues, we should not naively trust our observations, either in astronomy or in assessing the capacities of women.

2 Descartes had argued that we do not need to assume the existence of a 'soul' or 'form' in animals in order to explain their behaviour; instead we should think of non-human animals as very complex machines and try to explain their sensations and their behaviour mechanically. Hence the so-called theory of animal machines, to which Poulain alludes here. The theory provoked many objections in the seventeenth century, primarily because it seemed to point in the direction of a similarly mechanistic explanation of human behaviour which would make human souls redundant.

3 The term '*philosophe*' is used here to mean someone who is familiar with the physical theory or natural philosophy of the period. Louis de Lesclache, in *Les advantages que les femmes peuvent recevoir de la Philosophie, et principalement de la Morale* (Paris, 1667), distinguishes three senses of the term '*philosophe*'; those who 'ordinarily teach in the schools [i.e. scholastic philosophers]' (p. 17), those who pursue natural philosophy and conduct

experiments after the manner of Jacques Rohault, and finally those who seek true wisdom as Lesclache understands it and learn to lead a morally good life.

4 The French text has: '*nous ne trouverions pas plus étrange de les voir sur les Fleurs de Lys, que dans les boutiques*'. Furetière explains, in the entry for *lis*, that the expression '*assis sur les fleurs de lis*' was used in reference to judges exercising their function in a tribunal or, as one might say colloquially in English, sitting 'on the bench'. See Antoine Furetière, *Dictionaire Universel* (The Hague and Rotterdam: Arnout & Reinier Leers, 1690).

5 The picture of a Golden Age is repeated less hypothetically in *De l'excellence des hommes*, Part II, p. 109: 'In the first epoch of the world — some shadow of which survives in the innocent love of shepherds and shepherdesses and in the pastimes of rustic life, as long as it is not disturbed by the fear of armies or enemies — all people were equal, just and honest, and they had no regulations or law apart from common sense.'

6 The text refers to sending men to the *école des Dames*, meaning to have them educated by the beneficial influence of women. Cf. F. Du Soucy, *Le Triomphe des Dames* (Paris, 1646), p. 108, where he claims that the conversation of women is the best school for the most polite (*honnête*) people.

7 Scholastic philosophy in the seventeenth century explained many natural phenomena by assuming the existence of mysterious faculties or forms which corresponded exactly to whatever phenomenon was to be explained and which were named after the phenomenon in question. For example, a piece of iron was said to attract iron filings because it had an 'attractive faculty', or a sleeping powder was said to put someone to sleep because it had a 'dormitive power'. Cartesians argued consistently that these were pseudo-explanations which only gave the appearance of understanding the phenomenon to be explained. Here Poulain refers to the *faculté coctrice* or 'digestive faculty'; food was assumed to be heated in the stomach and in that way it was digested. Thus if the *faculté coctrice* were operating properly, it would be a sign of good health. The

faculté coctrice was a typical pseudo-explanation which purported to explain changes in one's health.

8 William Harvey (1578–1657) was the author of the theory of blood circulation in *De motu cordis et sanguinis in animalibus* (1628). Descartes endorsed the claim by Harvey that the blood circulated through the arteries and veins and that the circular movement was explained by the pumping action of the heart; however, he disagreed with Harvey's explanation of how the heart beats, claiming that it contradicted the observed facts and that it was akin to the pseudo-explanations mentioned in the previous note. Cf. Descartes, *Discourse on Method*, part v, *The Philosophical Writings of Descartes* (Cambridge University Press, 1985), I, p. 136; D. Clarke, *Descartes' Philosophy of Science* (Manchester University Press, 1982), pp. 149–55. Despite Descartes's endorsement, at the time when Poulain was writing the official position of medical teaching in France was still opposed to accepting the theory of blood circulation.

9 Scholastic philosophers distinguished between the capacities which normally result from the nature of something, and extraordinary qualities which normally transcend something's nature. Since God is the creator of the nature of each thing, such as it is, the question was asked whether God could add on an extra property to the nature of something; for example, could God enable something which is purely material, such as a stone, to think? Such superadded properties were called obediential, since the nature of each thing was completely subject to God's commands and could be forced to assume properties which were miraculous or extraordinary.

10 This refers to medicines prescribed by officially recognised physicians, who traditionally looked to Hippocrates as their model of ideal medical practice in ancient times.

11 In this paragraph Poulain takes a position on two related issues which had been discussed by Cartesian natural philosophers in the latter part of the seventeenth century. First, he denies the validity of astrological explanations of meteorological phenomena. Once Cartesians

adopted the new Copernican astronomy, they either rejected astrology completely, as Poulain does here, or else they tried to provide mechanical explanations of how the planets could interact with the earth and thereby affect the tides, weather conditions, etc. The latter alternative was adopted, for example, by the Cartesian philosopher Claude Gadroys, in his *Discours sur les influences des astres, selon les principes de M. Descartes* (Paris, 1671), which attempted to substitute — in place of current astrology — a mechanical, astronomical theory to explain the influence of planets and stars on natural phenomena on earth. The second issue considered by Poulain was the extent to which astronomical phenomena might influence the health or behaviour of human beings; here too he rejected astrological speculation and the kind of astronomical theory which Gadroys proposed. Poulain argued, in *De l'éducation des dames* (p. 301), that we do not know enough about human behaviour to be in a position to decide if it is affected or not by distant planets.

12 The text has *cause nécessaire* which is more naturally translated, in this context, as a sufficient or adequate cause.

13 St Vincent de Paul and St Louise de Marillac founded the religious order of sisters called the Daughters of Charity in 1633, with a special mission of visiting the poor and sick and taking care of them in their own homes; the idea of religious sisters working outside a convent in the homes of the poor was a novel idea in the seventeenth century.

14 The Hôtel-Dieu was a hospital near Notre Dame in Paris which cared especially for indigent sick patients. In 1634 St Vincent de Paul introduced the Ladies of Charity to assist the religious sisters of the Hôtel-Dieu; the Ladies of Charity were lay auxiliaries, including many ladies of noble rank, who devoted their time to works of charity in their parishes. The literature about women's status in the 1640s and 1650s often extolled the virtues of the heroic woman, the *femme forte*; in this paragraph Poulain adopts the same language about the *femme forte* to describe those who worked in the Hôtel-Dieu.

15 The phrase 'gallery of heroic women' reflects one of the standard genres of writing in favour of women in the period, which combined illustrations of women renowned for virtue (e.g. Judith in the Old Testament) and a discussion of the virtues for which they were famous. See for example P. le Moyne, *La Gallerie des Femmes fortes* (Paris, 1647), or M. de Scudery, *Les femmes illustres, ... avec les veritables portraits des ces Heroines, tirez des Medailles Antiques* (Paris, 1642).

16 The two prejudices in question are: (a) that those who are generally thought be to learned deserve to be believed; (b) that women are inferior to men. The first prejudice helps to reinforce the second one to the extent that the opinion of learned people coincides with popular prejudice.

17 Jean-François Sarasin (1615–54), sometimes spelled Sarazin; *Les oeuvres de M. Sarasin* were published in Paris in 1656, and reprinted two years later in Rouen. Poulain alludes to the sonnet, *A Monsieur de Charleval*:

> Lors qu'Adam vit cette jeune beauté
> Faite pour luy d'une main immortelle,
> S'il l'aima fort, elle de son costé
> (Dont bien nous prend) ne luy fut pas cruelle.
>
> Cher Charleval, alors en verité
> Ie croy qu'il [*sic*] fut une femme fidelle,
> Mais comme quoy ne l'auroit-elle esté,
> Elle n'avoit qu'un seul homme avec elle.
>
> Or en cela nous trompons tous deux,
> Car bien qu'Adam fût jeune et vigoureux,
> Bien fait de corps & d'esprit agréable.
>
> Elle aima mieux pour s'en faire conter,
> Prester l'oreille aux fleuretes du Diable,
> Que d'estre femme & ne pas caqueter.
>
> *Les oeuvres du Monsieur Sarasin* (Rouen: Augustin Courbé, 1658), p. 61.

Sarasin's poem could be translated as follows:

> When Adam saw the young beauty
> Created by an immortal hand for him

He loved her very much, and she reciprocated —
For which we are lucky — and returned his love.

Dear Charleval, I believe that truthfully
She was a faithful wife
But how could she have been otherwise
When she only had one man in paradise.

But we are mistaken in thinking this;
For although Adam was young and vigorous,
Sound in body and of a pleasant disposition,

She preferred to be courted and to listen
To the sweet nothings of the Devil,
Than to be a woman and not gossip.

18 The Amazons were frequently quoted in the literature of the period both in support of women and, in the opposite direction, to prove how badly women behave when they exercise power. For example, Rolet argues, in *Tableau historique des ruses et subtilitez des femmes* (Paris, 1623), pp. 12–13:

> There is no one who has not heard of the tyrranical domination of the Amazons, who expelled all the men from their country and were so barbaric even towards their own children that, when they gave birth to a male child, they immediately killed him, thereby showing their desire to expand their tyrannical empire and to prevent any man becoming king.

19 A reference to the contract theory of political authority which was prevalent in the seventeenth century and is usually associated with the name of Hobbes and, later, Locke. According to this theory, individuals in a state of nature (a hypothetical condition prior to the political organisation of people into commonwealths) would voluntarily associate and form a binding contract to provide mutual help to each other in order to facilitate realising basic aims such as self-preservation and security. They would also establish some person or some group of people with authority to enforce the terms of the contract on participating individuals. The political authority of their ruler(s) therefore derived completely from the freely assumed contract of the individuals.

20 The argument that men are not impartial in judging women, because they are both judge and a party to the case, was originally used by an obscure author who is only known as Captain Vigoureux, who replied to an extremely misogynist tract on women written by Olivier in 1617 (see Introduction above). Captain Vigoureux replied, in *La defence des femmes, contre l'Alphabet de leur pretendue malice & Imperfection* (Paris, 1617), p. 154: 'It is true that many authors have slandered women, but to sit in judgement on their claims would be to make men both judge and litigant at the same time, which is forbidden by the laws of man.'

21 This refers to the Areopagite Council of Athens, which exercised various judicial functions from the sixth century BC; these functions changed considerably with the changing fortunes of the Areopagus. In Poulain's text, the Areopagus is a symbol of ideal justice.

22 The Moors were Mohammedan natives of a region of North Africa which corresponds to parts of modern Morocco and Algeria. Both Turks and Moors were considered to be equally barbarian; thus acting like a Turk to a Moor is acting like a barbarian.

23 *Etres de raison* are things which do not exist in reality but only in the mind; they exist only in the sense that we think about them.

24 This is a reference to the Cartesian theory of ideas, according to which ideas of natural phenomena occur in all of us in the same way (assuming our senses are functioning properly), and they occur without any effort on our part. All we have to do is to open our eyes in order to see, or to listen in order to hear. By contrast, the ideas of artificially produced phenomena, such as embroidery, can only be acquired by a slow, difficult training process.

25 The suggestion that the mind or soul have no sexual characteristics is not unique to Poulain. It derives from the Cartesian distinction of mind and body into two completely different substances, so that sexual characteristics belong only to the body. The same idea is found, for example, in Christina of Sweden, *Ouvrage de Loisir ou maximes et sentences de Christine reine de Suède*, in

Mémoires pour servir à l'histoire de Christine reine de Suède, 2 vols. (Amsterdam and Leipzig: Mortier, 1751), vol. 1, p. 26: 'It is true that the soul has no sex.' See also P. Le Moyne, *La Gallerie des Femmes fortes* (Paris, 1647), p. 250: 'one must say boldly and without fear of harming it that philosophy has no sex, no more than intellects; that the true philosophy came for women just as much as men and, being the crowning perfection of the mind and the completion of reason, all reasonable souls are equally capable of its discipline'.

26 Descartes devoted his last major work to an examination of the passions; see *The Passions of the Soul* (1649), reprinted in the standard Adam and Tannery edition as vol. XI of *Oeuvres* (Paris: Vrin, 1964–74). Descartes argued notoriously that the human soul and body are such that one is spiritual and the other is material and that, despite the fact that they are different substances, they interact in some inexplicable way in human beings. Thus we can have thoughts in our mind which cause our bodies to move, and our bodies can suffer physical effects which cause appropriate experiences in the mind. Descartes adopted the traditional distinction between actions and passions in order to describee various mental events as either causes or effects of something else; thus the mind is *active* as cause of its own decisions, while it is *passive* when something acts on it and gives rise to some effect in the mind. The term 'passion' was reserved for those experiences which occur in the mind as effects of some causal agent. This would include cases where the mind causes itself to have other mental events, for example, when we perceive the fact that we have made a decision (in which case, the perception is a passion); however, the standard example of a passion for Descartes is when the mind is affected by something taking place in the body (which, in turn, is often caused by some external stimulus). Descartes's general definition was: 'those perceptions, sensations or emotions of the soul which we refer particularly to it, and which are caused, maintained and strengthened by some movement of the [animal] spirits' (*Philosophical Writings of Descartes*, ed. J. Cottingham,

R. Stoothoff and D. Murdoch: Cambridge University Press, 1985; I. pp. 338–9).

27 Here Poulain assumes, following Descartes, that there is a single scientific method which applies equally to every intellectual enterprise; this is the method suggested by Descartes in his *Discourse on Method* (1637).

28 Gazettes were periodicals which became popular in France in the seventeenth century. The first and most famous was the *Gazette* founded by Théophraste Renaudot in 1631, which was a weekly publication of 8 to 12 pages; it provided a forum for discussion of political, religious and artistic news and also gave summaries of what the editor considered to be interesting news from abroad. The *Gazette* was also used by Renaudot to disseminate news of discussions in the *Bureau d'Adresse*, an informal academy which, among other things, provided a venue for scientific discussions prior to the founding of the *Académie royale des sciences* in 1666. More generally, the word '*gazette*' referred to a weekly publication which gave news from different countries. Livy was a celebrated classical author of a history of Rome, *Ab urbe condita*, and Quintus Curtius Rufus was the first-century AD author of *The History of Alexander the Great of Macedon*.

29 The argument proposed here is not entirely clear from the text. Poulain wishes to argue that the mere possession of riches is not enough to make a miser happy, nor is knowing that he has riches enough; whether he is satisfied or not depends on his desires. If a miser desired merely to have riches in the immediate present, then knowing that he has them would make him happy. However, if he desired to retain his riches for a long time into the future, the knowledge that he might lose them at some later stage is enough to make him unhappy. Thus knowledge is always a necessary condition for the miser being happy, but it is not a sufficient condition because it depends on what the miser desires. The kind of knowledge which Poulain defends as equally important for men and women is not like this.

30 *Parlement*, a French institution which had judicial and, to some extent, legislative functions in the seven-

teenth century. Its original and principal function was similar to that of a high court or supreme court, deciding some cases as a court of first instance and acting as a court of final appeal for others. It also had the function of registering the king's edicts or letters patent; it could veto these if it found that they were inconsistent with the law and in this way it could delay their implementation; however the king could also force the *parlement* to register his edicts.

31 This paragraph alludes to the informal study-circles or *salons* which proliferated in the seventeenth century, especially in Paris, and which provided the only venue for women to discuss scientific, literary or similar topics; while the *salons* were ridiculed by many as pretentious, Poulain defends them as the only outlet available to women in a society in which they were precluded from the official academies, such as the *Académie française* or the *Académie royale des sciences.*

32 The Cartesian theory of sensation, implicit in this paragraph, assumed that the senses are physically stimulated by small particles of matter (or, in some cases, impulses) which travel from objects and then strike our senses; these physical impulses are transmitted to the brain which, in turn, causes the mind to have the appropriate feeling or sensation. Poulain's point is that women's senses are more sensitive in being able to register the effects of very feeble or very fast moving particles which might escape detection by those of a less sensitive disposition.

33 *Honnêteté*: the concept of an *honnête femme* was contested in the period in which Poulain was writing. *Honnêteté* was an ideal of social conduct which, in the case of women, was primarily defined in terms of the virtues which women were expected to cultivate, especially chastity and other virtues which expressed submission (such as humility, piety, etc.). The inner virtue associated with female *honnêteté* was manifest in the norms of behaviour according to which a woman ought to conduct herself in polite society. St Francis de Sales, in his *Introduction to the Devout Life*, had a significant influence on

combining the secular ideal of polite social behaviour with a Christian ideal of married life, so that *honnêteté* in Poulain's time included both the Christian virtues which were thought to be appropriate to women and a model of conduct in polite society. I have translated the words *honnête* and *honnêteté* in this paragraph as propriety, decency, respectability (and their adjectival equivalents), according as one or other word seemed more appropriate in the context.

34 The debate about propriety or decency during the period when Poulain published his work addressed the general issue of whether natural functions were indifferent and whether standards of propriety were mere human conventions which could change from one country or culture to another. Moise Amyraut, in the Preface to *Considerations sur les droits par lesquels la nature a reiglé les marriages* (Saumur, 1648), argued against the thesis that 'everything is indifferent in nature and the distinctions which we make are nothing but a silly custom of nations . . .'. On pp. 77–81 he considers the case of animal and human excretion to illustrate the demands of propriety.

35 Cartesians supported a preformation theory according to which all subsequent generations of any living creature, both plants and animals, are already included in embryo in the first members of the species. Thus the female ova already contain the woman's children in miniature, and her children's children, and so on; the role of the male in conception is limited to stimulating the development of these ova, by analogy with the function of rain in the propagation of plants from seeds.

36 In Article II of *Essai des remarques particulieres sur la langue françoise, pour la ville de Geneve*, Poulain lists misuses of French words, among them (pp. 14–15) the word '*feminin*' when used to mean weak or delicate.

37 This is possibly a reference to P. du Bosc, *L'Honneste Femme* (Paris, 1632), which provides an analysis of the advantages and disadvantages of different types of temperament; in chapter 1, 'De l'humeur gaye & melancholique', he claims that the first type of temperament is

best for conversation and social graces, whereas the second type is more appropriate for kings and philosophers (p. 22).

38 The various faults which were characteristically attributed to women were not invented by Poulain. It is evident from contemporary discussions that these were some of the standard faults which writers attributed to women. See for example Fénelon, *On the Education of Girls*, Chapters IX and X, where he discusses curiosity, diffidence, affectation, jealousy, inordinate friendships, loquaciousness, proneness to tears, false modesty, craftiness, and the 'chief fault' of women, namely vanity.

39 A reference to the Aristotelian theory that each virtue is half-way between two vices which represent the condition of having too much or too little of the quality in question; for example, bravery is the mean between cowardice and temerity.

40 A reference to the commonplace attributed to Plato, on the basis of *Timaeus* (91 A–D); see Introduction above, note 17.

41 In *On the Generation of Animals* (728a 18–20), Aristotle claims that women are deformed males. 'A woman is as it were an infertile male; the female in fact is female on account of inability of a sort, viz., it lacks the power to concoct semen out of the final state of the nourishment ... because of the coldness of its nature.' (Translated by A. L. Peck; Loeb Classical Library, London: Heinemann, 1942.)

42 Diogenes Laertius reports, in his *Lives of Eminent Philosophers*, VI, p. 52, the following comment of Diogenes about women: 'Seeing some women hanged from an olive-tree, he said, "Would that every tree bore similar fruit".' (English translation by R. D. Hicks; London: Heinemann, 1979, vol. 2, p. 53).

43 Tabarin is the pseudonym of Antoine Girard or Jean Salomon (1584–1633), the prototype buffoon whose stories and farces were published in Paris in 1622. *Verboquet le généreux* is the pseudonymous author of stories and comedies, published in Paris in 1630, which were supposed to cheer up melancholy people. Espiègle is a fictional character renowned for knavish jokes. The stories of Tabarin and Verboquet were notoriously bawdy; Poulain is suggesting that people would think much more positively of them if, instead of being contemporaries, they had been writing in the time of Diogenes. Age alone would give them an air of respectability similar to the ridiculous sayings of the philosophers.

Index

WITHDRAWN
UNIVERSITY LIBRARY